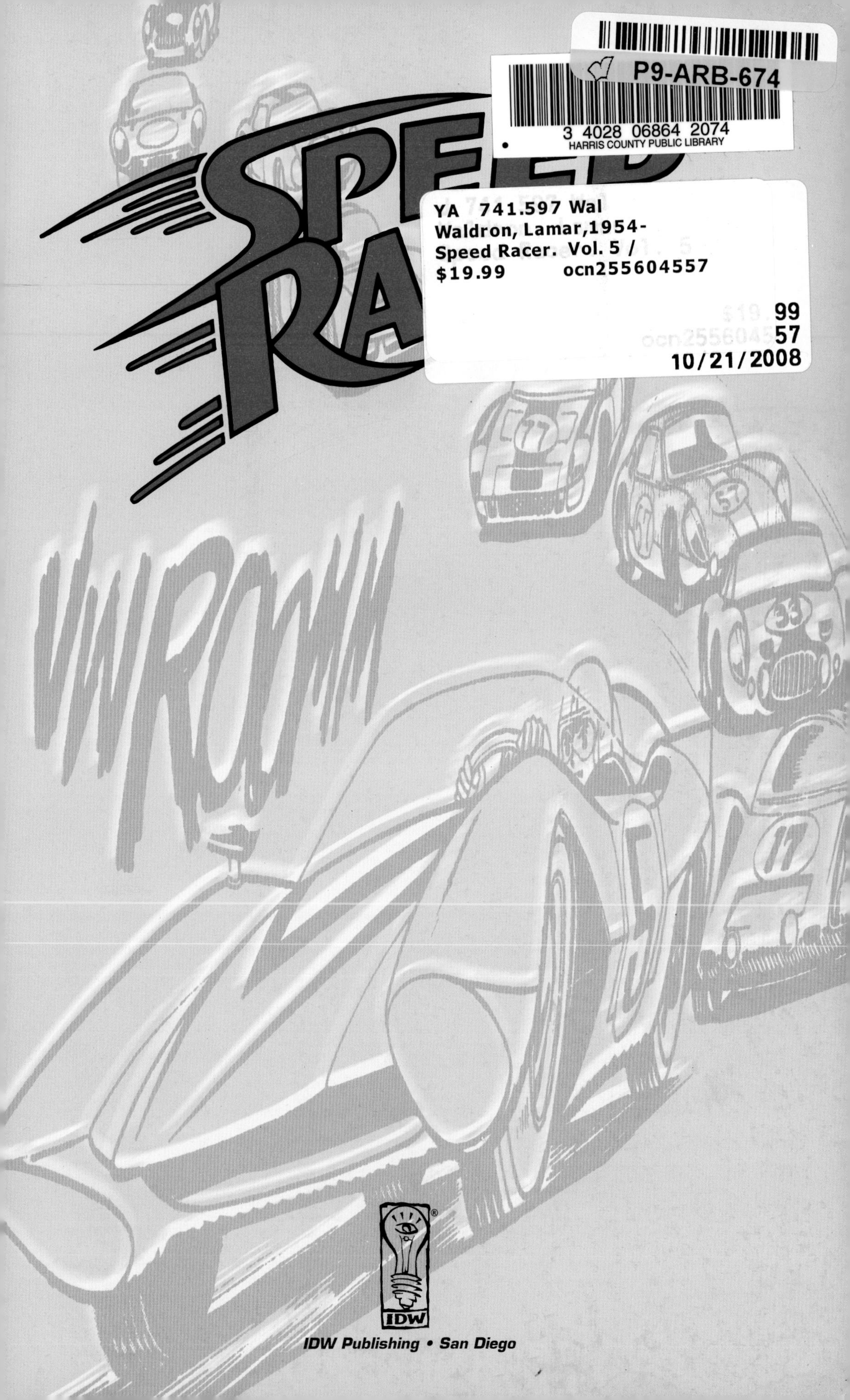
P9-ARB-674
3 4028 06864 2074
HARRIS COUNTY PUBLIC LIBRARY
YA 741.597 Wal
Waldron, Lamar,1954-
Speed Racer. Vol. 5 /
$19.99 ocn255604557
99
57
10/21/2008

IDW Publishing • San Diego

IDW Publishing
Operations:
Ted Adams, President
Moshe Berger, Chairman
Clifford Meth, EVP of Strategies
Matthew Ruzicka, CPA, Controller
Alan Payne, VP of Sales
Lorelei Bunjes, Dir. of Digital Services
Marci Kahn, Executive Assistant
Alonzo Simon, Shipping Manager

Editorial:
Chris Ryall, Publisher/Editor-in-Chief
Justin Eisinger, Editor
Andrew Steven Harris, Editor
Kris Oprisko, Editor/Foreign Lic.
Denton J. Tipton, Editor
Tom Waltz, Editor

Design:
Robbie Robbins, EVP/Sr. Graphic Artist
Neil Uyetake, Art Director
Chris Mowry, Graphic Artist
Amauri Osorio, Graphic Artist

www.idwpublishing.com
www.speedracer.com

ISBN: 978-1-60010-178-6
11 10 09 08 1 2 3 4 5

Speed Racer Volume 5, MAY 2008. FIRST PRINTING. © Speed Racer Enterprises, Inc., 2008. All rights reserved. TM and ® "SPEED RACER" is trademark of Speed Racer Enterprise, Inc. and is used under license. IDW Publishing, a division of Idea and Design Works, LLC. Editorial offices: 5080 Santa Fe Street, San Diego, CA 92109. Any similarities to persons living or dead are purely coincidental. The IDW logo is registered in the U.S. Patent and Trademark Office. All Rights Reserved. With the exception of artwork used for review purposes, none of the contents of this publication may be reprinted without the permission of Idea and Design Works, LLC. Printed in Korea.
IDW Publishing does not read or accept unsolicited submissions of ideas, stories, or artwork.
This volume collects Now Comics Speed Racer issues #26 to 31.

Speed Racer #26
page 5
Written by ***Lamar Waldron***
Pencilled by ***Norm Dwyer***
Inked by ***Jim Brozman***
Lettered & Colored by
Dan Nakrosis

Speed Racer #27
page 28
Written by ***Lamar Waldron***
Pencilled by ***Norm Dwyer***
Inked by ***Jim Brozman***
Lettered by ***Dan Nakrosis***

Speed Racer #28
page 51
Written by ***Lamar Waldron***
Pencilled by ***Norm Dwyer***
Inked by ***Jim Brozman***
Lettered by ***Dan Nakrosis***

Speed Racer #29
page 74
Written by ***Lamar Waldron***
Pencilled by ***Norm Dwyer***
Inked by ***Jim Brozman***
Lettered by ***Dan Nakrosis***

Speed Racer #30
page 96
Written by ***Lamar Waldron***
Pencilled by ***Norm Dwyer***
Inked by ***Brian Thomas***
Lettered by ***Patrick Williams***
Colored by ***Joseph Allen***

Speed Racer #31
page 119
Written by ***Lamar Waldron***
Pencilled by ***Norm Dwyer***
Inked by ***Brian Thomas***
Lettered & Colored by
Joseph Allen

Speed Racer Vol. 5

Edited by ***Justin Eisinger***
Design and Remaster by ***Tom B. Long***

Speed Racer #26

"THEY CALL IT THE CITY OF ANGELS... BUT THE VISITORS ROOM OF THE COUNTY JAIL DIDN'T REMIND ME OF HEAVEN. MY NAME IS SPEED RACER AND I KNEW THAT IF I DIDN'T CLEAR MY GIRLFRIEND TRIXIE OF HER BOGUS MURDER RAP, SHE'D BE FACING REAL ANGELS ALL TOO SOON. WHETHER YOU GET IT FROM AN ELECTRIC CHAIR OR ANOTHER INMATE, IT'S STILL...
the LONG SLEEP
I TRIED TO CALL YOUR PARENTS, TRIXIE! BUT THEY'RE CELEBRATING THEIR ANNIVERSARY BY TAKING ALL THEIR FRIENDS ON AN EXPEDITION UP THE AMAZON!
THE AUTHORITIES ARE TRYING TO REACH THEM-- BUT THEY SAID IT WOULD TAKE AT LEAST A WEEK!
OH SPEED, I CAN'T STAND IT IN HERE ANOTHER MINUTE! YOU DON'T KNOW HOW AWFUL IT IS, BEING LOCKED UP LIKE AN ANIMAL IN A CAGE...
--- WITHOUT A SHRED OF DIGNITY! I CAN'T BELIEVE THIS IS HAPPENING TO ME!
LAMAR WALDRON WRITER
NORM DWYER PENCILS & COVER
JIM BROZMAN INKS
DAN NAKROSIS LETTERS & COLORS
MICHELE MACH ART DIRECTOR
KATHERINE LLEWELLYN EDITOR
TONY CAPUTO EDITOR-IN-CHIEF

MY PARENTS ARE WORTH MILLIONS! THEY OWN STOCK IN EVERYTHING FROM GENERAL AUTO-MOTIVE TO MAJESTIC PICTURES---
---AND I CAN'T EVEN AFFORD A GOOD ATTORNEY WHO CAN GET ME OUT ON BAIL!
53

WELL, I'M GOING TO DO EVERYTHING I CAN TO GET YOU OUT OF HERE! NOW, TELL ME EVERYTHING YOU CAN REMEMBER ABOUT THE, UH--

MURDER? I'VE TOLD THE DETECTIVES OVER AND OVER TILL I'M SICK OF IT. BUT IF YOU THINK IT'LL DO ANY GOOD, HERE'S WHAT HAPPENED...

"MARLO McGEE, A FRIEND I'D KNOWN IN BOARDING SCHOOL, HAD INVITED ME TO LOS ANGELES FOR A VISIT. WE'D GONE TO THE GOLDEN APPLE NIGHTCLUB TO TALK OVER OLD TIMES..."
THIS PLACE IS BEAUTIFUL, MARLO-- LIKE SOMETHING OUT OF AN OLD MOVIE!
I THOUGHT YOU'D LIKE IT, TRIXIE! HAVE YOU EVER SEEN ANOTHER PLACE THAT HAS OVER FIFTY VARIETIES OF MINERAL WATER?

IF YOU'LL EXCUSE ME A MOMENT, I'VE GOT TO "FRESHEN UP", AS THEY USED TO SAY!

EXCUSE ME, MISS! I COULDN'T HELP BUT NOTICE HOW LOVELY YOU ARE! WOULD YOU LIKE TO DANCE?
NO THANKS-- THIS IS STRICTLY A GIRLS NIGHT OUT!

OH, COME ON! MY NAME'S LENNOX-- TERRY LENNOX-- AND I'M A VERY GOOD DANCER!

NO! AND THAT'S FINAL!

I LIKE WOMEN THAT PLAY HARD TO GET-- BUT YOU'VE RESISTED LONG ENOUGH!

LOOK, BUDDY, SINCE MY WORDS AREN'T GETTING THROUGH TO YOU, MAYBE THIS WILL!

IS HE BOTHERING YOU, MISS? I'M BILL-- THIS IS MY CLUB AND I WON'T LET MY CUSTOMERS BE HARRASSED!
SORRY! I--I WON'T BOTHER THE YOUNG LADY ANYMORE!

MOMENTS LATER...
YOU MISSED ALL THE EXCITEMENT!
MAYBE THIS IS A GOOD TIME TO LEAVE! I KNOW ANOTHER PLACE THAT'S A LOT OF FUN!

GOLDEN APPLE CLUB
I CAN'T BELIEVE THE NERVE OF THAT GUY!
SOME GUYS JUST DON'T KNOW WHEN TO TAKE NO FOR AN ANSWER!

OOPS! I MUST HAVE LEFT MY WALLET IN THE CLUB! WAIT HERE--I'LL BE RIGHT BACK!

A FEW MINUTES LATER...
I WISH MARLO WOULD HURRY... I DON'T LIKE WAITING OUT HERE ALL ALONE!
LUB

LOOK, BEAUTIFUL, I WANT TO--
YOU AGAIN! GET AWAY FROM ME-- OR I'LL SCREAM!

"SUDDENLY, I HEARD THE MUFFLED SOUND OF GUNFIRE, AS HE DOUBLED OVER IN PAIN! THERE WERE FIVE, MAYBE SIX SHOTS... I CAN'T REMEMBER FOR SURE!"
UUUUGH!

"I DON'T KNOW HOW LONG I STOOD THERE, LOOKING AT HIS LIFELESS, BLEEDING BODY, BEFORE I STARTED TO..."

...SCREAM!"

TRIXIE! WHAT'S WRONG?
HE-- HE'S-- DEAD!

WAS HE THE MAN WHO WAS BOTHERING YOU? DID YOU SHOOT HIM?
H-HE'S THE MAN-- BUT I DIDN'T KILL HIM!

I HEARD SHOTS!
THERE'S THE BLONDE WHO RAN OUT OF THE CLUB WHEN THE SHOOTING STARTED! MAYBE SHE SAW WHO DID THE SHOOTING!

SORRY OFFICER, BUT I DIDN'T SEE WHO FIRED THE SHOTS! IS HE--?
HE'S DEAD, ALL RIGHT! YOUR FRIEND LOOKS PRETTY SHAKEN UP! DID SHE SEE ANYTHING?

LOOK!--GUN SHELLS! SHE MUST HAVE SHOT HIM!
NO! I DIDN'T DO IT!

I'D LIKE TO BELIEVE YOU, MISS--- BUT THAT GUN BEHIND YOU MAKES IT AWFULLY HARD! I'M PLACING YOU UNDER ARREST! YOU HAVE THE RIGHT TO REMAIN---

LOS ANGEL
HEIRESS KILLS PLAYBOY
BOYFRI
SPEED
RAC
STUN
TRIXIE SAYS SHE'S INNOCENT
EPI—World famous hieress Trixie Van Derbucks was arrested early this morning at the trendy Golden Apple Club.
A shattered Trixie Van Derbucks hides in shame as police lead her from the scene of the crime in handcuffs.
this morning. Golden
patrons continued to party the night away. One jaundiced patron said, "I am just glad
THE POLICE GAVE ME A PARAFIN TEST, TO SEE IF I HAD TRACES OF GUNPOWDER FROM FIRING THE PISTOL! I DON'T KNOW HOW, BUT IT CAME OUT POSITIVE!
VISITING HOURS ARE OVER! YOU'LL HAVE TO COME WITH ME, NOW!
I KNOW YOU'RE INNOCENT, TRIXIE --- AND I'LL FIND A WAY TO PROVE IT!

MY FRIEND MARLO IS A PRIVATE DETECTIVE! SHE'S LOOKING FOR EVIDENCE THAT'LL CLEAR ME -- WILL YOU HELP HER?
I'LL DO EVERYTHING I CAN!

THE CASE AGAINST TRIXIE SEEMS AIRTIGHT... BUT I KNOW SHE COULD NEVER DO SUCH A THING! IT JUST DOESN'T MAKE SENSE...
EXIT
YOU'LL HAVE TO WAIT A MOMENT SIR, UNTIL THESE NEW PRISONERS ARE OUT OF THE HALLWAY!
HOLDING CELLS
CELL BLOCK
C

WELL, IF IT ISN'T MY OLD FRIEND, SPEED --THE JERK WHO FINGERED ME FOR THE COPS!
SATIN TURANA! I THOUGHT YOU WERE IN CHICAGO!

THEY EXTRADITED ME BACK HERE ON AN OLD CHARGE--FOR STABBING ANOTHER PRISONER!
YOU KNOW SPEED--

--I'M REALLY GOING TO ENJOY MY STAY IN JAIL THIS TIME! 'CAUSE I'LL HAVE TRIXIE TO KEEP ME COMPANY!
STAY AWAY FROM HER!

DON'T WORRY, SPEED! I'LL TAKE GOOD CARE OF TRIXIE, FOR THE REST OF HER LIFE, --WHICH WON'T BE LONG! HA! HA! HA! HA!
YOU CAN'T PUT HER IN THERE WITH TRIXIE!

DON'T BE RIDICULOUS! WHERE ELSE WOULD WE PUT HER?
AT LEAST LET ME WARN TRIXIE!
SORRY, SIR--VISITING HOURS ARE OVER!

"AN HOUR LATER, I WAS AT PAUL TRUMAN'S HOME IN BEL AIRE HILLS..."
IT WAS NICE OF PAUL TO LET ME STAY AT HIS PLACE WHILE HE'S AWAY ON LOCATION. IT GIVES ME A GOOD BASE...
...FOR ALL THE WORK I HAVE TO DO! FIRST, I NEED TO CALL INSPECTOR DETECTOR! HE OWES ME A FAVOR--

HELLO? IS THIS INTERPOL? I NEED TO SPEAK WITH INSPECTOR DETECTOR! TELL HIM IT'S URGENT!
I'M SORRY, SIR! THE INSPECTOR IS ON ASSIGNMENT IN INDIA! WOULD YOU LIKE TO LEAVE A MESSAGE?

OH WELL... MAYBE POPS OR SPARKY CAN COME DOWN FROM SAN FRANCISCO TO HELP OUT! I'LL CALL HOME...

NO, SON, YOUR FATHER'S NOT HERE! HE AND SPARKY ARE WORKING ON THOSE NEW TIRES FOR THE MACH 5! HE WANTS THEM READY FOR NEXT WEEK'S RACE IN SEATTLE!

WINNING THERE IS OUR ONLY WAY TO RAISE MONEY FOR TRIXIE'S DEFENSE! POOR GIRL-- THIS MUST BE AWFUL FOR HER!

I GUESS IT'S ALL UP TO ME... AND TRIXIE'S FRIEND MARLO!
IT'S ALMOST FIVE O'CLOCK! MAYBE SHE'S STILL AT HER OFFICE...

"MARLO'S OFFICE WAS IN A RUNDOWN OFFICE BUILDING IN A RUNDOWN PART OF HOLLYWOOD. HER DETECTIVE WORK MUST NOT PAY VERY WELL..."
WHAT DO YOU THINK OF THE CASE THE POLICE HAVE AGAINST TRIXIE?
THE PARAFIN TEST WAS CONCLUSIVE-- AND THE BULLET SHELLS WERE THE SAME TYPE USED IN THE PISTOL THEY FOUND BEHIND TRIXIE!

EVEN THOUGH THE BULLETS WERE TOO FRAGMENTED FOR BALLISTICS TO MATCH THEM PRECISELY TO THE PISTOL...

-THEIR CASE IS GOING TO BE HARD TO BEAT! IT DOESN'T LOOK GOOD!

SOMEONE MUST HAVE SET UP TRIXIE TO MAKE HER LOOK GUILTY! THAT'S THE ONLY ANSWER!
DOES SHE HAVE ANY ENEMIES? MAYBE--

"SUDDENLY MY EARS STARTED RINGING, AND I FELT SHARDS OF GLASS PIERCE MY SKIN AS SOMEBODY BEGAN USING MARLO'S OFFICE WINDOWS FOR TARGET PRACTICE..."
CRASH!
BANG!
BANG!
QUICK! GET DOWN!

I'M GLAD ALL THE OTHER PRISONERS HAVE FINISHED... I JUST CAN'T STAND TO BATHE AROUND SUCH DANGEROUS CHARACTERS!

WELL, WELL-- WHAT HAVE WE HERE? A FISH OUT OF WATER?
SATIN!

COME BACK HERE!
STAY AWAY FROM ME!

I'VE GOT A SCORE TO SETTLE WITH SPEED! I CAN'T GET TO HIM-- BUT I'VE GOT YOU RIGHT WHERE I WANT YOU!

THINK HOW SAD HE'D BE IF YOU HAD A LITTLE ACCIDENT!

SATIN-- LET THE KID GO! YOU KNOW THE RULES!
I WOULDN'T DREAM OF HURTING HER---AT LEAST NOT IN FRONT OF WITNESSES!
I'LL NEVER GET OUT OF HERE ALIVE!

"WHEN THE FIRING STOPPED, I WAS AMAZED TO FIND THAT NEITHER ONE OF US WAS HURT! THEN, MARLO MADE A DECOY, TO SEE IF IT WAS SAFE TO HEAD FOR THE DOOR..."

BANG
BANG!

"SO WE SAT TIGHT FOR A FEW HOURS, TRADING LIFE STORIES TO PASS THE TIME..."
I NEVER REALLY KNEW MY FATHER, BUT HE SENT ME TO THIS EXPENSIVE SCHOOL IN SWITZERLAND!
THAT'S WHERE I MET TRIXIE!
I HAD TO DROP OUT WHEN HE DIED AND THE CRASH OF '87 WIPED OUT MY INHERITANCE!

ALL I HAD LEFT WERE DAD'S HOUSEBOAT AND AN OLD CAR THAT SOME CLIENT HAD GIVEN HIM. DAD WAS SORT OF A DETECTIVE--

--SO I CAME TO CALIFORNIA AND GOT INTO THE SAME BUSINESS!
NO SHOTS! THE COAST IS CLEAR!

SPEED, I KNOW YOU WANT TO HELP, BUT YOU'D BE A LOT SAFER IF YOU'D LEAVE THE INVESTIGATING TO ME! BESIDES, I'VE ALREADY INTERVIEWED ALL THE WITNESSES!
THERE MUST BE SOME WAY I CAN HELP!

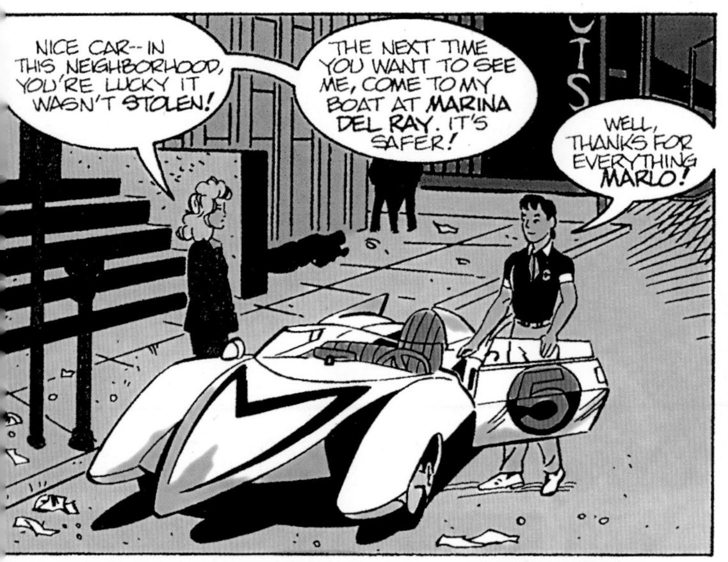
NICE CAR-- IN THIS NEIGHBORHOOD, YOU'RE LUCKY IT WASN'T **STOLEN**!
THE NEXT TIME YOU WANT TO SEE ME, COME TO MY BOAT AT **MARINA DEL RAY**. IT'S SAFER!
WELL, THANKS FOR EVERYTHING **MARLO**!

I'VE GOT TO DO SOMETHING... AT LEAST GO TO THE **SCENE OF THE CRIME** AND LOOK AROUND...

"A FEW MINUTES LATER, I WAS AT THE **GOLDEN APPLE CLUB**. WITHOUT A TIE, I FELT EXTREMELY UNDERDRESSED. BUT, **BILL**, THE OWNER, WAS VERY HELPFUL..."
WHEN YOU RUN A CLUB, YOU HEAR ALOT OF TALK-- AND WORD WAS THAT **LENNOX** WAS BEING PRESSURED TO SELL HIS INTEREST IN A **MOVIE STUDIO** TO SOME GANGSTERS.

EVERYONE I TALKED TO SAID THAT LENNOX HAD ALWAYS BEEN POLITE WITH WOMEN. THE WAY HE ACTED TOWARD TRIXIE JUST DOESN'T MAKE SENSE.

IT SURE DOESN'T! DID YOU TELL ALL OF THIS TO MARLO?
THE BLONDE WHO WAS WITH TRIXIE? I HAVEN'T SEEN HER SINCE THE SHOOTING.

HOW COULD MARLO OVERLOOK TALKING TO BILL? I'D BETTER LOOK AROUND... SHE MIGHT HAVE OVERLOOKED SOME OTHER CLUES!
GOLDEN APPLE
MACH V

THIS MUST BE WHERE THE VICTIM WAS HIT... AND SINCE TRIXIE DIDN'T SHOOT HIM, THE SHOTS MUST HAVE COME FROM FURTHER AWAY!
POLICE LINE DO NOT
CROSS

SOMEONE COULD HAVE FIRED FROM BEHIND THAT FENCE...

THE EVIDENCE WAS ARRANGED SO THE POLICE IMMEDIATELY SUSPECTED TRIXIE... BUT A PERSON WITH A TELESCOPIC SIGHT COULD HAVE EASILY HIT LENNOX FROM HERE!

WAP
WHAT TH--

I CAN'T BELIEVE THIS! A NINJA IN L.A.?
PREPARE TO DIE!

SOME WARRIOR... HIS BLADE'S STUCK IN THE FENCE!

HE'S TOO CLUMSY TO BE A REAL NINJA! MY BROTHER REX TAUGHT ME ENOUGH ABOUT MARTIAL ARTS TO TAKE CARE OF HIM!

OKAY--TALK! MY GIRLFRIEND'S LIFE IS IN DANGER, AND I'LL---

"SUDDENLY, I FELT A BLOW FROM BEHIND...
UUGGHH!!

"I FELT LIKE SOMEONE SLIPPED A BLACK VELVET GLOVE OVER MY HEAD, AS MY CONSCIOUSNESS SLOWLY FADED AWAY..."

"I AWOKE TO THE SOUNDS OF SEA GULLS AND THE SMELL OF SALT WATER..."
WELCOME ABOARD! IT'S A GOOD THING I DROPPED BY THE GOLDEN APPLE TO SEE BILL, OR I MIGHT NOT HAVE FOUND YOU!
I'M GLAD YOU DID!
HOUSE

PLEASE DON'T GET MIXED UP IN ALL OF THIS! I LIKE YOU TOO MUCH--
--TO SEE YOU GET HURT! WHY, I'VE BEEN AN ADMIRER OF YOURS FOR A LONG TIME!

OH, SPEED DARLING, EVER SINCE TRIXIE USED TO BRAG ABOUT YOU, BACK IN SCHOOL..-

--I'VE WANTED TO SHOW YOU HOW I REALLY FEEL!

MONTROSE ST.
GOSH, MARLO, I DIDN'T REAL-IZE IT WAS SO LATE! I'D BETTER BE GOING!
WAIT-SPEED!

YOUR CAR'S STILL AT THE CLUB! COME BACK AND I'LL DRIVE YOU!
NO, THANKS! I'LL TAKE A CAB!

N HOUR LATER, I WAS BACK AT PAUL'S...
THE PHONE! I HOPE IT'S NOT MARLO...
RING! RING!

INSPECTOR DETECTOR! THANKS FOR RETURNING MY CALL! TRIXIE'S IN TROUBLE AND...
NO NEED TO EXPLAIN, SPEED! IT JUST MADE THE PAPERS HERE IN INDIA!

I CAN BE IN L.A. IN THREE DAYS! UNTIL THEN, I'LL ARRANGE FOR YOU TO ACCESS THE INTERPOL CRIME FILES THROUGH PAUL'S COMPUTER, TO SEE IF YOU CAN FIND ANY LEADS!

IT'S AGAINST REGULATIONS--BUT IT'S THE LEAST I CAN DO AFTER YOU HELPED ME BUST THAT DRUG RING!

THANKS, INSPECTOR! I JUST HOPE I CAN FIGURE OUT HOW TO USE PAUL'S COMPUTER!

"LUCKILY, PAUL HAD THE KIND OF COMPUTER I COULD LEARN TO USE IN LESS THAN AN HOUR..."
TOP YOUNG GUN
TRUMAN
LENNOX OWNED LOTS OF STOCK IN MAJESTIC STUDIOS ...AND I REMEMBER TRIXIE SAYING THAT HER FOLKS OWNED STOCK IN THAT COMPANY, TOO!

CREAK!

WHO'S TH--?

NOW, YOU WILL DIE!

NOTHING TO USE AS A WEAPON ...EXCEPT MY CHAIR!

I SHOULDN'T ATTACK WHILE HE'S STILL GOT THE GUN... BUT IT'S MY ONLY CHANCE TO GET EVIDENCE TO CLEAR TRIXIE!

"BUT AFTER A SHORT ROLL AROUND THE TERRACE, I LEARNED THAT A CLUMSY NINJA CAN STILL BE DANGEROUS AS LONG AS HE HAS AN AUTOMATIC..."
WAIT! BEFORE YOU KILL ME, I HAVE TO KNOW ---WHY WAS TRIXIE SET UP? PLEASE!

YOU THINK I AM A CLUMSY FOOL! BUT I SHOT LENNOX--- SO THAT YAKUZA FROM MY PARENTS HOMELAND COULD BUY HIS SHARES IN MAJESTIC STUDIOS!
MY PARTNER AND I---

--- WILL BLACKMAIL TRIXIE'S PARENTS INTO GIVING UP THEIR SHARES IN MAJESTIC, IN RE-TURN FOR EVIDENCE TO CLEAR THEIR DAUGHTER!

HEY, SPEED!
HUH?

HE'S LOST HIS BALANCE!

HE DIED, GOING FOR THE GUN! I'LL BET THAT GUN... OR ONE LIKE IT, WAS USED TO KILL LENNOX! AND NOW, IT'S GONE...
WHAT'S GOING ON SPEED?

I'LL CALL THE POLICE, AND THEN EXPLAIN EVERYTHING! BUT FIRST, I NEED A QUICK ACTING LESSON FROM YOU!
ACTING LESSON? I DON'T UNDERSTAND...

"TWO HOURS LATER..."
MARLO-- I'M SORRY FOR THE WAY I ACTED! I REALLY WANT TO TALK TO YOU!
SURE! COME ON IN!

I'VE THOUGHT ABOUT WHAT YOU SAID THIS MORNING! IT'S HARD FOR ME TO SAY THIS, MARLO, BUT--I FEEL THE SAME WAY ABOUT YOU!
OH, SPEED!

I ONLY GO WITH TRIXIE BECAUSE OF HER MONEY! BUT EVEN THOUGH YOU'RE NOT RICH, I CARE FOR YOU MORE THAN I EVER CARED FOR TRIXIE!

I- I ALMOST WISH TRIXIE WOULD NEVER GET OUT OF JAIL, SO WE COULD ALWAYS BE TOGETHER!
YOU DON'T KNOW HOW HAPPY I AM TO HEAR YOU SAY THAT!

OH--WHAT'S THE USE? TRIXIE'S PARENTS WILL TURN UP SOON, AND GET TRIXIE OUT ON BAIL!
AND I'LL HAVE TO PRETEND TO STILL CARE FOR HER, SO SHE'LL KEEP FINANCING MY DRIVING CAREER!
IT DOESN'T HAVE TO BE LIKE THAT, SPEED!

SOON, I'LL HAVE ENOUGH MONEY FOR BOTH OF US! NOW THAT I KNOW HOW YOU REALLY FEEL, I CAN TELL YOU THE WHOLE STORY!

I HAD BEEN WORKING ON TRIXIE TO VISIT ME FOR WEEKS! I KNEW LENNOX WOULD BE AT THE CLUB THAT NIGHT---

"...AND I TOLD HIM THAT TRIXIE WAS DYING TO MEET HIM. I SAID SHE'D PLAY HARD TO GET, IN CASE ANY GOSSIP COLUMNISTS WERE AROUND, BUT THAT HE SHOULD BE PERSISTENT!"

"YOU SHOULD HAVE SEEN LENNOX'S FACE WHEN SHE THREW HER WATER ON HIM!"

"AFTER LEAVING TRIXIE AT THE CAR, I TOLD LENNOX THAT TRIXIE WAS REALLY SORRY FOR WHAT SHE'D DONE AND THAT SHE WANTED TO APOLOGIZE TO HIM..."

"MY PARTNER, HASHIMIRO, HAD ALREADY PLANTED THE GUN! I'D ALREADY FIRED IT EARLIER THAT DAY, SO I COULD LEAVE TRACES OF GUNPOWDER ON TRIXIE'S ARM..."

YOU WOULDN'T BELIEVE HOW MUCH HASHIMIRO'S GANGSTER FRIENDS ARE PAYING US TO HELP THEM GAIN CONTROL OF MAJESTIC STUDIOS!
WE'LL BOTH BE RICH!

THE WORST PART WAS HAVING TO CONK YOU OVER THE HEAD! BUT YOU WERE GETTING TO THE TRUTH! OH, DARLING NOW WE CAN...

YOU'RE UNDER ARREST!
WHAT!?

"MY PLAN WORKED LIKE A CHARM... THE POLICE HEARD EVERYTHING! MARLO'S CONFESSION COULDN'T BE USED IN COURT, BUT IT WAS ENOUGH TO CLEAR TRIXIE. AND I WAS SURE A SEARCH OF MARLO'S BOAT WOULD TURN UP ENOUGH EVIDENCE TO PUT HER AWAY FOR A LONG TIME!"

OH, SPEED --WHY? WE COULD HAVE HAD SUCH A BEAUTIFUL LIFE TOGETHER!
A LIFE OF CRIME ISN'T MUCH OF A LIFE, MARLO!
THE END.

Speed Racer #27

WAIT! LISTEN-- I'M NOT A DEMON! I'M A HUMAN, NAMED SPEED RACER! AND THAT MACHINE ISN'T EVIL-- IT'S MY CAR, THE MACH 5! CAN'T YOU UNDERSTAND?
DON'T LISTEN TO THE WARLOCK! HE LIES!
QUICKLY, NOW--- PUT HIM AND HIS INFERNAL DEVICE TO THE TORCH, BEFORE HE POISONS YOUR MINDS!
WITCH HUNT
LAMAR WALDRON SCRIPT
NORM DWYER PENCILS, COVER
JIM BROZMAN INKS
DAN NAKROSIS LETTERS
COLORS
KATHERINE LLEWELLYN EDITOR
MICHELE MACH ART DIRECTOR
TONY CAPUTO EDITOR-IN-CHIEF

YOU FOOLS--- WHEN THE FLAMES HIT THE MACH 5'S GAS TANK, THE EXPLOSION WILL KILL US ALL!
THIS IS ALL SO CRAZY... AS IF I'VE GONE BACK IN TIME!
"IT'S HARD TO BELIEVE THAT ONLY THIS MORNING, I WAS STANDING WITH TRIXIE ON THE BEACH AT OLYMPIC NATIONAL PARK...
OH, SPEED--- IT'S SO BEAUTIFUL HERE! I WISH WE COULD STAY ALL DAY!
ME TOO! BUT I NEED TO BE IN SEATTLE BY THIS AFTERNOON, TO HELP POPS AND SPARKY FINISH TESTING THE NEW TIRES THEY INSTALLED FOR THE RACE!
LOOK! SOMEONE IS CLINGING TO THAT JAGGED ROCK!
YOU'RE RIGHT! HIS BOAT MUST HAVE RUN AGROUND!

HE'S NOT EVEN WEARING A LIFE JACKET!
IN THESE ROUGH WATERS, HE'LL NEVER MAKE IT TO SHORE!

HE NEEDS HELP--AND FAST!

BE CAREFUL, SPEED!

BY CLOSING THE CANOPY AND ACTIVATING MY UNDERWATER TURBO THRUSTERS, I CAN DRIVE RIGHT OUT TO HIM!
CLICK!

UH-OH! I CAN HEAR ROCKS SCRAPING THE BOTTOM OF THE CAR! I'D BETTER BE CAREFUL, OR THEY MIGHT PUNCTURE MY OIL PAN!

THIS IS A GOOD TIME TO TEST MY NEW TIRES! IF I CAN OVER-INFLATE THEM...
CLICK!
CLICK!

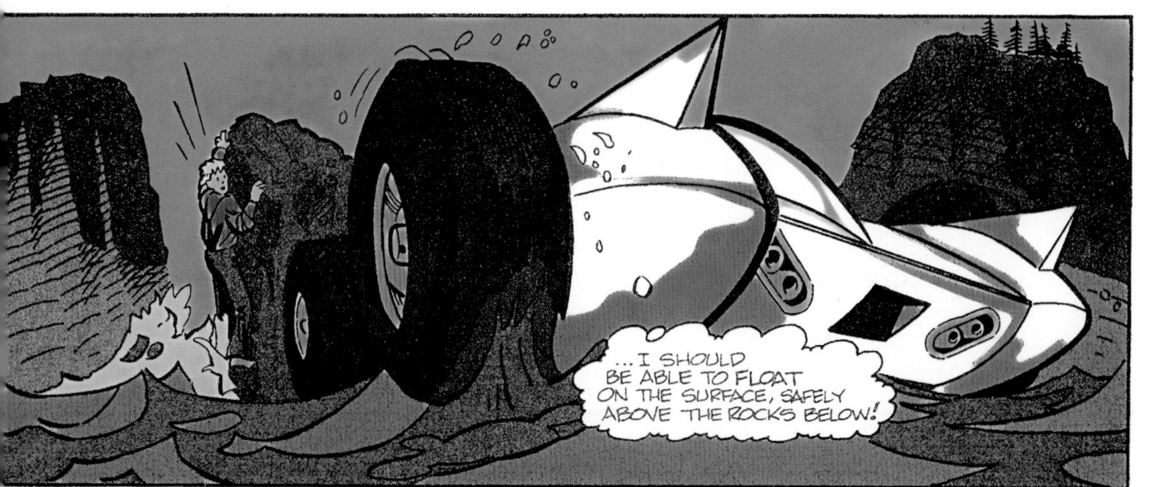
...I SHOULD BE ABLE TO FLOAT ON THE SURFACE, SAFELY ABOVE THE ROCKS BELOW!

MOMENTS LATER...
S-STAY AWAY FROM ME, SEA DEMON!
HE MUST BE DELIRIOUS, FROM EXHAUSTION...
GRAB MY HAND! QUICK, BEFORE ONE OF THESE WAVES--

SPLASH!
I'M GLAD THAT WAVE KNOCKED ME TOWARD THE MACH 5... OR I'D NEED RESCUING, TOO!

THE WAVES ARE GETTING HIGHER BY THE MINUTE... NO TIME TO LOSE!
CLICK!

OH NO! MY FOOT MUST HAVE HIT THE CANOPY BUTTON!

SPLASH!
THIS WATER'S FREEZING! MUSCLES ARE CRAMPING FROM THE COLD... HAVE TO REACH THE CAR...

SPEED! SPEED!
I MADE IT! BUT THE CAR IS FLOATING AWAY FROM SHORE!

THIRTY MINUTES LATER...
I CAN'T SEE THE COAST AT ALL... JUST AN OCCASIONAL SHARK!
THERE'S AN EMERGENCY CANOPY RELEASE UNDERNEATH THE CAR... BUT IT'S TOO RISKY TO TRY AND REACH IT!

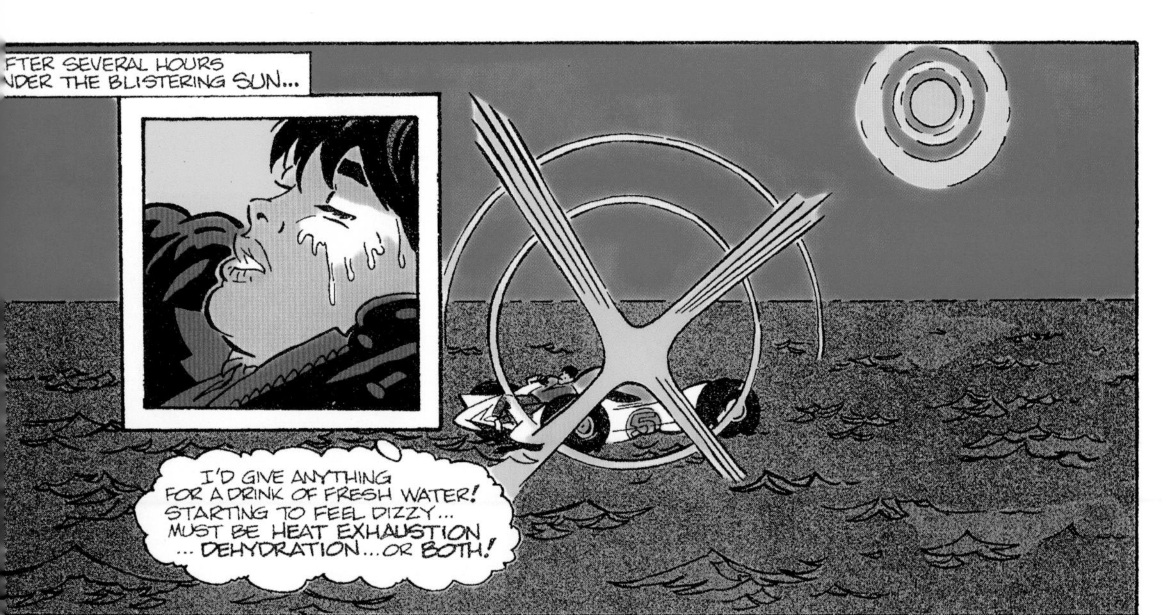
FTER SEVERAL HOURS
NDER THE BLISTERING SUN...
I'D GIVE ANYTHING FOR A DRINK OF FRESH WATER! STARTING TO FEEL DIZZY... MUST BE HEAT EXHAUSTION ... DEHYDRATION... OR BOTH!

HAVE TO STAY ALERT AND AWAKE ...OR I MIGHT LOSE MY GRIP ON THE CAR!

ON THE HORIZON... IS IT A MIRAGE?

AN ISLAND! IT LOOKS REAL ENOUGH... AND THE CURRENT'S TAKING ME STRAIGHT TO IT!

HIRTY MINUTES LATER...
AS SOON AS I GET THE CAR ASHORE, I'LL POP THE MANUAL CANOPY RELEASE AND RADIO FOR HELP!

UH-OH... HERE COMES A WELCOMING COMMITTEE! I WONDER WHO LIVES HERE?

THEY LOOK LIKE THEY'VE SEEN A GHOST--YOU'D THINK THEY'D NEVER SEEN A CAR BEFORE! AND WHY ARE THEY WEARING THOSE OLD-FASHIONED CLOTHES?

SPEAK UP LAD --WHO ARE YOU? WHAT MANNER OF SEA SERPENT HAVE YOU CAUGHT?

MY NAME IS SPEED RACER---BUT I DON'T KNOW ANYTHING ABOUT A SEA SERPENT!

WAIT A MINUTE! YOU MEAN MY CAR!

THIS IS NO SEA MONSTER! LOOK--

--IT'S AN AUTOMOBILE! DON'T YOU UNDERSTAND? IT'S JUST A MACHINE, WITH AN ENGINE, AND--
A MACHINE!
QUICKLY--SEIZE THIS WARLOCK, BEFORE HE KILLS US ALL!

NO! WAIT! WHAT ARE YOU DOING?
PROTECTING OUR FAMILIES FROM THE EVIL OF MACHINERY!

MINUTES LATER...
WHERE AM I? THIS VILLAGE LOOKS LIKE IT BELONGS IN THE 1800'S! IS IT A TOURIST ATTRACTION?
I KNOW NOT OF TOURISTS! YOU ARE IN NEW SALEM-- THE LAST REFUGE OF THE UNCORRUPTED!

THIS OUTSIDER HAS BROKEN THE LAW! HE WAS FOUND WITH A MACHINE AND MUST SURELY BE A PRACTITIONER OF BLACK MAGIC!
YOU'RE CRAZY!!

MY SON--SAMUEL HAS DISAPPEARED! WE'VE SEARCHED THE WHOLE ISLAND!
THE OUTSIDER, HAS, NO DOUBT, USED HIS MACHINE TO SPIRIT HIM AWAY!
THIS HAS GONE FAR ENOUGH! I DEMAND THAT YOU RELEASE ME!

SILENCE, OUTSIDER! MY AUTHORITY COMES FROM MRS. ALCOTT, WHO OWNS THE ENTIRE ISLAND! HER FAMILY HAS ALWAYS MADE THE LAW--AND AS JUDGE, I ENFORCE IT!

MACHINES HAVE ALWAYS BEEN FORBIDDEN IN NEW SALEM! MECHANICAL DEVICES DESTROY THE LAND AND DIRTY THE SKY! THEY ARE EVIL---

---AND THOSE WHO USE THEM MUST PAY THE ULTIMATE PRICE! I SENTENCE YOU, SPEED RACER, TO BE BURNED AT THE STAKE!

A SHORT TIME LATER...
THAT'S RIGHT--- PUSH THE MACHINE ONTO THE KINDLING! IT MUST BE DESTROY-ED ALONG WITH ITS MASTER!
WAIT! I JUST REALIZED--- I KNOW WHERE THE MISSING BOY IS!
I'M SURE YOU DO, DEMON WARLOCK!

THE JUDGE HAS THEM SO WORKED UP THAT THEY WON'T LISTEN TO ANYTHING!

THE HEAT IS UNBEARABLE! I CAN'T LAST MUCH LONGER...

EANWHILE, BACK AT OLYMPIA NATIONAL PARK...
I'M GLAD I WAS ABLE TO FLAG YOU DOWN! BUT WHAT ABOUT SPEED? HAVE ANY BOATS SPOTTED THE MACH 5?
NOT YET! AND I'M AFRAID IT'S TOO LATE TO SEND A SEARCH PLANE OUT TODAY-- BUT WE'LL HAVE ONE OUT LOOKING FOR HIM FIRST THING IN THE MORNING!

CAN I USE YOUR RADIO? I NEED TO CALL SPEED'S FAMILY!

AT SEATTLE INTERNATIONAL SPEEDWAY...
GO TEAM
SPEED AND TRIXIE SHOULD HAVE BEEN HERE HOURS AGO!
I HOPE NOTHING'S HAPPENED TO THEM!
LISTEN--- ISN'T THAT THE RADIO? I'LL SEE WHO IT IS!

WHAT'S WRONG SPARKY?
IT-- IT'S TRIXIE! SHE'S PRETTY UPSET... YOU'D BETTER TALK TO HER--

SPEED RACER
YOU MEAN THAT SPEED FLOATED OUT TO SEA ON THE MACH 5!?!? BUT, TRIXIE, HOW--
NO TIME TO EXPLAIN NOW, POPS! I NEED YOU TO START LOOKING FOR A HELICOPTER I CAN RENT--

THE FOLLOWING MORNING...
UH-- WHERE AM I? WHO ARE YOU? THE LAST THING I REMEMBER, THE JUDGE WAS HAVING ME BARBECUED!
I ORDERED HIM TO RELEASE YOU! MY NAME IS LAURA ALCOTT! MY FAMILY HAS OWNED-- AND RULED THIS ISLAND FOR OVER A HUNDRED YEARS!

WHEN MY GRANDFATHER AND HIS FOLLOWERS ARRIVED HERE, HE BANNED ALL MACHINERY FROM THE ISLAND--- BECAUSE OF THE WAY FACTORIES HAD RUINED AND POLLUTED HIS NATIVE NEW ENGLAND!

SURELY YOU MUST HAVE SOME CONTACT WITH THE OUTSIDE WORLD--
CARRIER PIGEONS KEEP ME IN CONTACT WITH A LAW FIRM IN SEATTLE! THEY ADMINISTER A TRUST FUND TO INSURE THAT MY ISLAND IS KEPT OFF MAPS-- AND IS LEFT UNDISTURBED.

LOOK, I JUST WANT TO GET TO SEATTLE FOR AN IMPORTANT RACE---
OUTSIDERS ARE NOT ALLOWED TO LEAVE! THOSE WHO ARE HEALTHY AND INTELLIGENT--

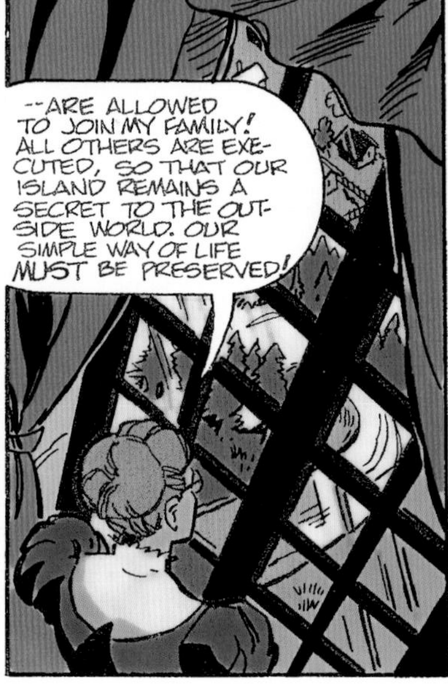
--ARE ALLOWED TO JOIN MY FAMILY! ALL OTHERS ARE EXECUTED, SO THAT OUR ISLAND REMAINS A SECRET TO THE OUTSIDE WORLD. OUR SIMPLE WAY OF LIFE MUST BE PRESERVED!

YOU MEAN YOU HAVE THEM KILLED? THAT'S BARBARIC!

I'M GETTING OUT OF THIS CRAZY PLACE RIGHT NOW!
YOU'LL NEVER FIND YOUR VEHICLE! AND REMEMBER, YOU'RE ON AN ISLAND, THERE'S NO PLACE YOU CAN HIDE FOR VERY LONG!

OH YEAH? WELL, I'D RATHER TAKE MY CHANCES THAN--
MOTHER, I--

OOOPS!

ER-UH-SORRY, MISS! I'M---
YOU'RE OBVIOUSLY A CLUMSY OAF!

THAT TEA SERVICE IS IRRE-PLACEABLE---AND YOU'VE BROKEN IT TO PIECES, YOU STUPID OUT-SIDER!

ELIZA! WATCH YOUR TONGUE! THAT'S NO WAY TO TALK TO YOUR FUTURE HUSBAND!
HUSBAND?
HUSBAND?

MEANWHILE...
THIS IS TRIXIE, CALLING SEARCHER ONE! WE'VE FINISHED WITH SECTOR SEVEN---

---AND WE'RE READY TO BEGIN SECTOR EIGHT! VISIBILITY IS EXCELLENT, BUT WE HAVEN'T SPOTTED HIM YET! PLEASE KEEP US POSTED---OVER AND OUT!
GO

POOR TRIXIE... SHE DIDN'T GET A WINK OF SLEEP LAST NIGHT! I'VE NEVER SEEN HER SO WORRIED! I'VE GOT TO TAKE HER MIND OFF OF SPEED---

GEE--I WONDER HOW THAT GUY YOU RESCUED IS DOING?
I DON'T KNOW---BUT I'LL RADIO THE HOSPITAL AND FIND OUT!

MOMENTS LATER...
IT'S REALLY STRANGE, TRIXIE! HE SEEMS TO BE HEALTHY ENOUGH--BUT HE'S SCARED TO DEATH OF THE SIMPLEST THINGS!
NO! GET IT AWAY FROM ME!
2001-2010
X-RAY
NURSES STATION
DON'T BE AFRAID! THEY'RE NOT GOING TO HURT YOU!

LATER THAT AFTERNOON...
A FINE JUDGE YOU ARE, MY DEAR HUSBAND--- LETTING MRS. ALCOTT HUMILIATE YOU IN FRONT OF THE WHOLE TOWN!
HUSH, WOMAN! YOU SPEAK BLASPHEMY!
MAYBE -- BUT SHE SPEAKS THE TRUTH!

FOLKS WON'T BE SO QUICK TO HEED YOUR RULINGS, NOW THAT THEY'VE SEEN THAT YOU'RE NOT INFALLIBLE!

NO! THEY MUST NEVER QUESTION MY AUTHORITY!

SOME PEOPLE MIGHT FEEL MY JUDGEMENTS HAVE WRONGED THEM... IF I APPEAR WEAK, THEY MIGHT DECIDE TO SEEK REVENGE!

I KNOW--THE DEMON WARLOCK FROM THE SEA HAS BEWITCHED MRS. ALCOTT! THAT'S WHY SHE REBUKED ME! WE MUST SAVE HER SOUL---EVEN IF HER BODY MUST DIE!

AS EVENING STARTS TO FALL...
WHILE YOU MAKE A FRESH BATCH OF BUTTER, YOU TWO CAN GET BETTER ACQUAINTED! AND I WANT TO HEAR NO MORE ARGUING! IS THAT UNDERSTOOD?
YES, MOTHER!
I'LL PRETEND TO COOPERATE... UNTIL I FIND OUT WHERE THEY'VE HIDDEN THE MACH 5!

I'M SORRY I'VE BEEN CROSS WITH YOU-- BUT I'M SO WORRIED ABOUT SAMUEL! I DON'T KNOW WHAT'S BECOME OF HIM!

I WANTED TO MARRY HIM--- BUT MOTHER FORBADE IT, SAYING THAT WE MUST ALWAYS REMAIN APART FROM THE TOWNSPEOPLE!

SHE SAYS MARRYING WOULD CAUSE HIS RELATIVES TO BICKER OVER POWER AND INFLUENCE--- BUT I DON'T CARE ABOUT THAT! I LOVE SAMUEL!

EVEN THOUGH THE VILLAGERS ARE TAUGHT TO FEAR THE SEA, SAMUEL HAD BEEN WORKING ON A RAFT, SO WE COULD LEAVE THE ISLAND. HE SAID HE WAS GOING TO TEST IT-- AND THEN HE DISAPPEARED!

DON'T WORRY--
I KNOW WHERE SAMUEL IS! I'LL TAKE YOU TO HIM--

YOU WILL?
--IF YOU'LL HELP ME FIND MY CAR!

MOMENTS LATER...
I FEEL GUILTY ABOUT NOT TELLING HER EVERYTHING... I HOPE THAT TRIXIE WAS ABLE TO SEE THAT SAMUEL GOT SAFELY TO SHORE!

ONCE THEY'RE SAFELY OUTSIDE...
I HEARD LOTS OF NOISE COMING FROM THE OLD BARN LAST NIGHT! I'LL BET THAT'S WHERE IT WAS TAKEN!
ARE YOU SURE IT WON'T HURT ME?
NO--IT ONLY DOES WHAT I TELL IT TO!

IT DOESN'T LOOK LIKE IT WAS DAMAGED TOO BADLY BY THE FIRE!
WHAT WILL YOU DO NOW?
OPEN HER UP!

BUT AFTER SPEED FINDS THE MANUAL CANOPY RELEASE JAMMED...
I NEED TOOLS TO GET IT OPEN! DO YOU HAVE A DRILL-- OR A SOCKET WRENCH?
WHAT ARE THOSE?

THESE ARE THE ONLY TOOLS WE HAVE!
OH WELL, I'VE NEVER WORKED ON A CAR USING A MAL-LET AND AWL --- BUT THERE'S A FIRST TIME FOR EVERY-THING!

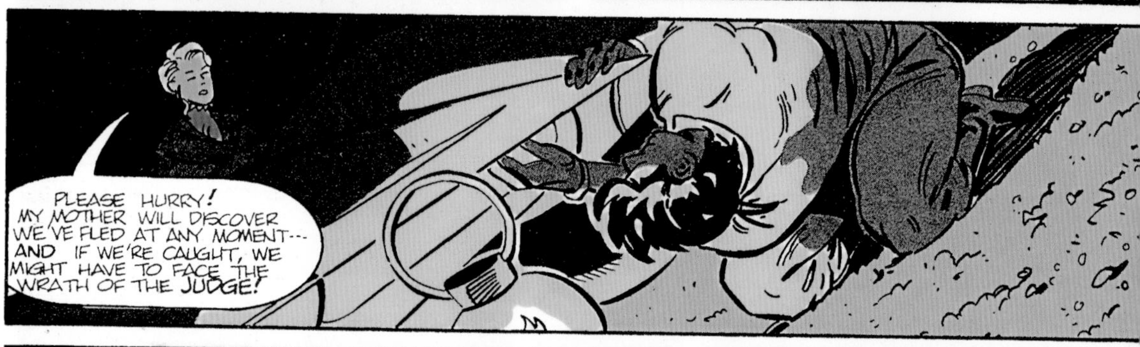
PLEASE HURRY! MY MOTHER WILL DISCOVER WE'VE FLED AT ANY MOMENT--- AND IF WE'RE CAUGHT, WE MIGHT HAVE TO FACE THE WRATH OF THE JUDGE!

MEANWHILE, IN THE VILLAGE...
THE DEMON AND HIS MACHINE HAVE BE-WITCHED MRS. ALCOTT! THEY'VE TURNED HER INTO ONE, A DEMON, TOO --AND THAT'S WHY SHE MADE ME RELEASE HIM!

YOUR FAMILIES WILL BE NEXT---UNLESS WE DESTROY ALL THE DEMONS, NOW!

THERE--- IT'S OPEN! BUT BEFORE I TAKE YOU AWAY FROM THE ONLY HOME YOU'VE EVER KNOWN, THERE'S SOMETHING I HAVE TO FIND OUT!

MAYDAY! MAYDAY! THIS IS SPEED RACER, MAYDAY--

IT'S TOO DARK TO LOOK ANYMORE, TRIXIE! WE'D BETTER HEAD IN---
NO, SPARKY! I'M GETTING A SIGNAL- IT'S FAINT, BUT IT SOUNDS LIKE SPEED!

MOMENTS LATER...
I'VE MISSED YOU, TOO, TRIXIE! BUT FIRST, I NEED TO KNOW IF THE YOUNG MAN I TRIED TO RE-SCUE IS SAFE!
HE'S FINE! BUT HOW ABOUT YOU, SPEED? ARE YOU ALRIGHT?

OH NOOO!

YOUR HOUSE!
MOTHER! SHE WAS--

QUICK--GET IN THE CAR! IT'S THE FASTEST WAY TO GET THERE!
I'M AFRAID! HOW CAN A MACHINE--?

NO TIME TO ARGUE!

YOU'LL BE ALL RIGHT--- I PROMISE!

WE'LL BE AT THE HOUSE IN **SECONDS**-- AND I'VE GOT **TWO EXTINGUISHERS** IN THE CAR!

SHE'S HIDING THE DEMON WARLOCK AND HIS EVIL MACHINE! IF SHE REFUSES TO TELL US WHERE THEY ARE-- THROW HER IN THE FIRE!
HE'S LYING! HAVE YOU ALL GONE MAD?

I AM THE ULTIMATE AUTHORITY HERE ON THE ISLAND!

DON'T YOU SEE--- THE DEMON HAS KILLED THE REAL MRS. ALCOTT! THIS IS AN IMPOSTER!

THE DEMON MUST BE DESTROYED!
STAY BACK! I GAVE YOU YOUR POWER---

WHAT MONSTER IS THIS?
RRROAR!

DIE, SPAWN OF HELL-- DIE!!

RUN FOR YOUR LIVES! THERE'S NO WAY TO STOP IT!

OH, MOTHER--
DID THEY
HURT YOU?
I'M
FINE,
DEAR.
YOU'RE SAFE FOR NOW, MRS. ALCOTT--- BUT SEEING MY CAR IN ACTION HAS PROBABLY CONVINCED THE VILLAGERS YOU'RE IN LEAGUE WITH THE DEVIL!

BUT I CAN MAKE SURE YOU'RE SAFE EVEN AFTER I LEAVE--- IF YOU'LL LET ELIZA MARRY SAMUEL AND CHANGE THE WAY THE ISLAND IS RULED!

I DON'T HAVE MUCH CHOICE, DO I?

LISTEN TO ME! ALL MACHINES ARE NOT EVIL! SOME CAN BE USED FOR GOOD! TO PROVE IT, I'LL HAVE A FLYING MACHINE BRING SAMUEL BACK BY MORNING!

SPEED TO TRIXIE--- I NEED THREE THINGS BY DAYBREAK! A CABLE STRONG ENOUGH TO HOIST THE MACH 5, THE YOUNG MAN YOU RESCUED-- AND A COPY OF THE U.S. CONSTITUTION!

HE FOLLOWING MORNING...
OH SPEED-- I'M SO GLAD YOU'RE SAFE! BUT WHAT IS THIS PLACE? WHY DOES EVERYTHING LOOK SO OLD?
IT'S A LONG STORY-- I'LL EXPLAIN ONCE WE'RE ALOFT!
OKAY, YOU LOVEBIRDS! SHE'S READY TO FLY!

THE WEDDING OF ELIZA AND SAMUEL WILL SIGNAL THE BEGINNING OF A NEW ERA ON THE ISLAND! NO LONGER WILL ONE MAN BE--

--JUDGE, JURY, AND EXECUTIONER! FROM NOW ON, WE'LL ALL SHARE THE RE-SPONSIBILITY OF GOVERNING NEW SALEM!

I WONDER IF I DID THE RIGHT THING? IT WOULD BE A SHAME TO SEE THE ISLAND SPOILED BY TOO MUCH PROGRESS!
LET'S JUST HOPE THEY'VE LEARN-ED TO USE STEAKS IN-STEAD OF STAKES AT THEIR NEXT COOKOUT!
The End

Speed Racer #28

MOON OF THE WOLF
SEATTLE INTERNATIONAL SPEEDWAY
"THE SEATTLE 1000"
ON THE LAST EVENING BEFORE QUALIFYING, SPEED RACER HAS BEEN RUNNING PRACTICE LAPS WITH HIS OLD FRIEND, CARL JACKSON, AND A NEW RACER FROM CANADA, LOU PINE...
HOW'D I DO, CARL?
YOU AND LOU FINISHED LESS THAN A TENTH OF A SECOND APART, SPEED! IF Y'ALL RUN THAT FAST TOMORROW, YOU'LL BREAK THE COURSE QUALIFYING RECORD!
IT LOOKS LIKE I REALLY HAVE TO WORK HARD TO KEEP UP WITH YOU TWO!
BLAME IT ON POPS AND SPARKY... THEY HAVE THE MACH 5 RUNNING BETTER THAN EVER!
LAMAR WALDRON STORY
NORM DWYER PENCILS
JIM BROZMAN INKS
DAN NAKROSIS LETTERS
THE STAFF COLORS
MICHELE MACH ART DIRECTOR
KATHERINE LLEWELLYN EDITOR
TONY CAPUTO EDITOR IN CHIEF

YOUR CAR'S RUNNING GREAT, TOO, LOU!
UH? OH- YEAH, RIGHT.

ARE YOU ALL RIGHT, LOU? YOU SEEM AWFULLY NERVOUS FOR SOMEONE WHO JUST DROVE A RECORD LAP!

IT'S JUST THAT I--- I DIDN'T REALIZE HOW LATE IT WAS.

LOU'S RIGHT! IT'S WAY PAST MY DINNER TIME! AFTER I FINISH CHECKING MY SUSPENSION, WOULD YOU GUYS LIKE TO GET SOME EATS?
SURE! HOW ABOUT YOU LOU--- ARE YOU HUNGRY?
YES-- BUT I'M AFRAID I'VE GOT OTHER PLANS.

OH, I GET IT! I HOPE YOU HAVEN'T KEPT HER WAITING TOO LONG!
ER, UH, SHE'S PROBABLY WONDERING WHAT'S KEEPING ME.

I'LL BET YOU'RE A REAL ANIMAL WITH THE GIRLS, LOU!
MORE THAN YOU KNOW, CARL!

HMMMM... I DON'T THINK LOU WAS REALLY NERVOUS ABOUT BEING LATE FOR A DATE!
HE WAS JUST PLAYING ALONG! SOMETHING HEAVY MUST BE ON HIS MIND!

SINCE LOU'S NOT JOINING US, MAYBE TRIXIE AND SPARKY WOULD LIKE TO COME ALONG!
GREAT IDEA! I'LL PICK THEM UP AT THE HOTEL---

---BE BACK HERE BY THE TIME YOU'RE FINISHED WITH YOUR SUSPENSION!
I'LL BE WAITING!

AFTER MOVING HIS CAR INTO THE PIT AREA...
SURE HOPE I CAN FIND OUT WHAT'S CAUSING THOSE VIBRATIONS... I DON'T WANT ANY DISTRACTIONS DURING QUALIFYING TOMORROW!

SPEED'S A GREAT GUY AND A GOOD FRIEND...

...BUT I'M STILL GOING TO DO MY BEST TO WIN! I'M SURE SPEED WILL DO THE SAME!

BAY 8 PIT
AND THAT GUY LOU ISN'T GOING TO BE EASY TO BEAT, EITHER!
GRRRR---
JAX

SPEED? IS THAT YOU?
...RROOO--

I DIDN'T THINK YOU'D BE BACK SO SOON!
---OOOWWW--

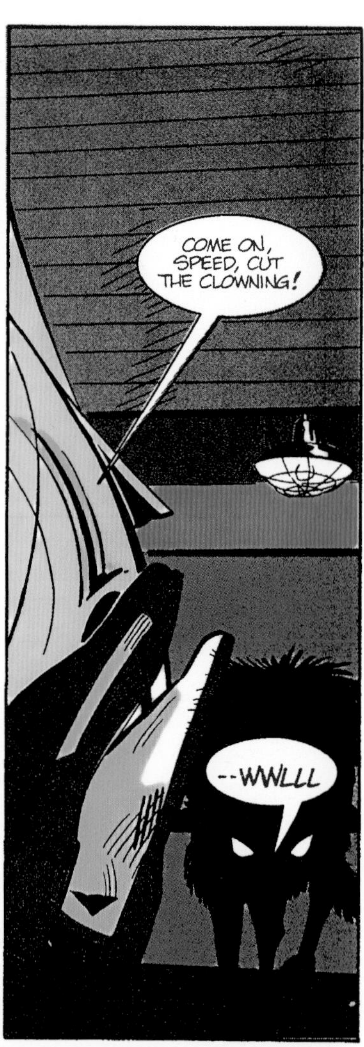
COME ON, SPEED, CUT THE CLOWNING!
--WWLLL

DON'T YOU KNOW IT'S RUDE TO GROWL?

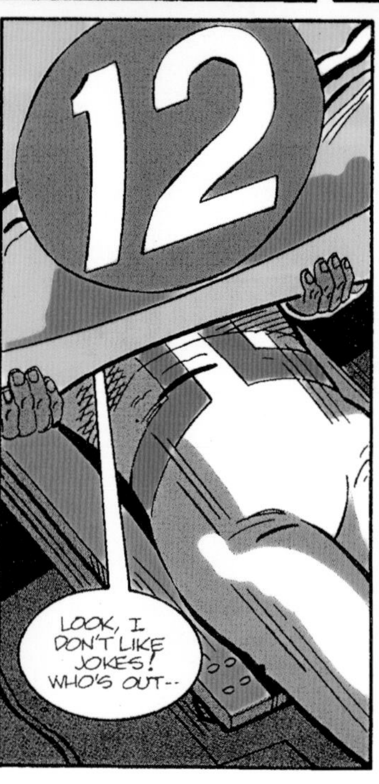
12
LOOK, I DON'T LIKE JOKES! WHO'S OUT--

--TH---TH--TH-

RROOARR!
YYYIIIAAA!

SNAP!!

CARL'S REFLEXES, HONED BY A FULL SEASON OF RACING, SPRING INTO ACTION AS HE SLIDES BACK UNDER THE CAR...
WHOOOSH!
THAT WAS CLOSE! I JUST HOPE...

...MY CAR'S CLEARANCE IS LOW ENOUGH TO KEEP THAT DOG... WOLF...OR WHATEVER IT IS, FROM GETTING A SECOND CHANCE!

RROOWWLL!!

HE'S SQUEEZING UNDERNEATH THE CAR! BUT IF I TIME IT JUST RIGHT...

...I SHOULD BE ABLE TO MAKE A RUN FOR IT...

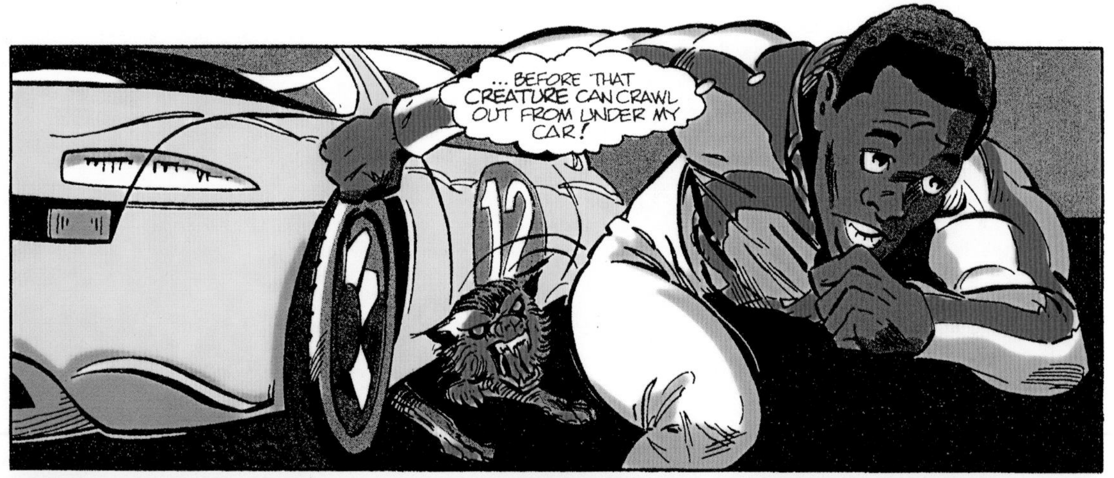
...BEFORE THAT CREATURE CAN CRAWL OUT FROM UNDER MY CAR!
12

OH, NO! IT'S MOVING QUICKER THAN I THOUGHT! THERE'S NO WAY I CAN OUT RUN IT!
PIT AREA
BAY 9
GOT TO TRY AND CLOSE THE INNER BAY DOOR...

...BEFORE THAT THING GETS ANOTHER CHANCE TO MAKE HAMBURGER OUT OF ME!

IT'S GETTING READY TO JUMP...

I DON'T BELIEVE IT! I'VE NEVER SEEN A CAR THAT COULD DENT ONE OF THOSE DOORS LIKE THAT!
WHUMP!!

WHATEVER IT IS, IT'S TRAPPED IN THERE WITH MY CAR! HOW CAN I GET IT OUT?

SHOULD I CALL THE POLICE? ANIMAL CONTROL? MAYBE SPEED'S BACK AT THE HOTEL ...HE'LL HELP ME FIGURE OUT WHAT TO DO!
SEATTLE 1000
OCTOBER

MOMENTS LATER, AT THE GO-TEAM'S SUITE...
HI, CARL! THIS IS SPARKY! NO, SPEED ISN'T BACK YET, BUT--WHAT!?
IT'S SOME TYPE OF MAD DOG! IT MUST BE CRAZY FROM RABIES, BECAUSE IT KEEPS BANGING AWAY, TRYING TO GET OUT!
WE'LL HEAD RIGHT OVER! I'LL RADIO SPEED FROM THE VAN, OKAY? CARL?
ARE YOU STILL THERE, CARL? WHAT'S WRONG?
KRASH!

FIFTEEN MINUTES LATER...
I HOPE THE POLICE GOT HERE IN TIME! DO YOU SEE SPEED ANYWHERE, SPARKY?
HE'S OVER HERE, TRIXIE!

BAY 8
SEATTLE AMBULANCE
WHERE'S CARL?
THEY--THEY'LL BE BRINGING HIM OUT SOON. BUT DON'T LOOK! YOU--YOU'LL NEVER BE ABLE TO GET IT OUT OF YOUR MIND!

I-- I HAD TO IDENTIFY WHAT WAS LEFT! IT-- WAS HORRIBLE!

OH, SPEED, HOW AWFUL!
I HAD ONLY BEEN GONE A FEW MINUTES, WHEN I GOT SPARKY'S CALL! BUT THOSE FEW MINUTES---

---WERE ALL IT TOOK FOR SOMETHING TO SNUFF OUT THE LIFE OF ONE OF THE BEST RACERS I'VE EVER KNOWN! IF ONLY I HADN'T LEFT HIM HERE, ALONE!

DON'T BLAME YOURSELF, SPEED! YOU COULDN'T HAVE KNOWN SUCH A TERRIBLE THING WOULD HAPPEN!

OFFICER, CARL SAID A WILD DOG--
NO DOG COULD DO ALL THIS! A GRIZZLY MAYBE--
--BUT WE DON'T HAVE BEARS RUNNING LOOSE IN SEATTLE! MAYBE THESE FUR SAMPLES CAN TELL US WHAT WE'RE UP AGAINST!

MEANWHILE, AT THE HOTEL WHERE LOU IS STAYING...
HOTEL INTERNATIONAL
WHAT... WHAT HAPPENED TO ME? HOW DID I WIND UP ON THE FLOOR...

...COVERED WITH BLOOD? IT'S THAT BLASTED FULL MOON... THE CURSE HAS STRUCK AGAIN!

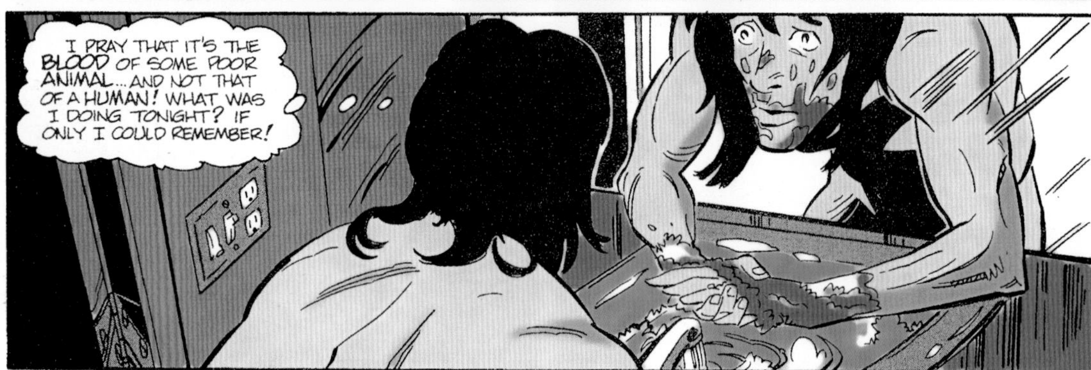
I PRAY THAT IT'S THE BLOOD OF SOME POOR ANIMAL... AND NOT THAT OF A HUMAN! WHAT WAS I DOING TONIGHT? IF ONLY I COULD REMEMBER!

KNOCK! KNOCK!
SOMEONE'S AT THE DOOR! IS IT THE POLICE?

SUE! THANK HEAVEN IT'S MY SISTER-- AND NOT THE AUTHORITIES!
WHAT'S WRONG? I CAME BY AN HOUR AGO, BUT YOU DIDN'T ANSWER! WHERE WERE YOU?

I'M--I'M NOT SURE! I CAN'T RECALL ANYTHING!
DON'T YOU REMEMBER? WE HAD DINNER TOGETHER--- BUT YOU WERE SO NERVOUS THAT YOU COULDN'T EAT! I'VE BEEN WORRIED ABOUT YOU!

THAT'S RIGHT! IT'S COMING BACK TO ME! AND BEFORE DINNER, I WAS AT THE TRACK--- WITH CARL AND SPEED! I HOPE THEY'RE ALL RIGHT!

WHY DO YOU SAY THAT? WHAT COULD HAVE HAPPENED TO THEM?
THERE'S A FULL MOON TONIGHT, SUE!

EVERY OCTOBER, IT'S ALWAYS THE SAME! WHEN THE MOON IS FULL, I HAVE BLACKOUTS AT NIGHT---

--AND AWAKEN THE NEXT DAY TO HEAR NEWS REPORTS OF HORRIBLE MURDERS NEARBY!
MAYBE IT'LL BE DIFFERENT THIS TIME, LOU! PERHAPS THE CURSE--

IF YOU'D SEEN THE BLOOD I WAS COVERED WITH, YOU'D KNOW THAT THE CURSE IS JUST AS STRONG AS EVER!

THE FOLLOWING DAY, AS SPEED GETS IN A FINAL PRACTICE LAP BEFORE QUALIFYING BEGINS...
00:37:56
DIGITECH
BLAST IT, SPEED YOU'RE GOING TOO SLOW! IF YOU DON'T GO FASTER DURING QUALIFYING, WE'RE IN BIG TROUBLE!
YOU'VE GOT TO---
GEE, POPS, TAKE IT EASY! HAVE YOU FORGOTTEN WHAT SPEED WENT THROUGH LAST NIGHT?
SEATTLE POST
RACER BRUTALLY SLAIN
HE HARDLY SLEPT A WINK, 'CAUSE HE KEPT HAVIN' NIGHTMARES ABOUT FINDIN' CARL'S BODY!
YOU'RE RIGHT, SPARKY! I'M SORRY, SON!
WE REALLY NEED THE FIRST PLACE PRIZE MONEY TO PAY OUR BILLS! BUT IF YOU DON'T FEEL LIKE RACING--
IT'S OKAY, POPS! I'LL BE ALL RIGHT!
IF ONLY I KNEW WHAT REALLY HAPPENED TO CARL! MAYBE LOU REMEMBERS SOMETHING...

SEVERAL MINUTES LATER...
HEY, LOU! I'D LIKE TO TALK TO YOU ABOUT LAST NIGHT...
WHAT'S THERE TO TALK ABOUT? I'VE ALREADY TOLD THE POLICE THAT I DIDN'T SEE THE WILD DOG THAT ATTACKED POOR CARL!
NO DOG COULD HAVE TORN THROUGH---
LOOK, SPEED, I'M REALLY BUSY!
I DON'T MEAN TO BE RUDE, BUT I'D RATHER NOT EVEN THINK ABOUT LAST NIGHT!
BUT MAYBE---
LEAVE MY BROTHER ALONE!
SUE-- PLEASE!!
SORRY, SPEED, I HAVE TO GO!
I CAN UNDER-STAND LOU BEING UPSET OVER CARL'S DEATH... BUT WHAT'S EATING HIS SISTER? THOSE TWO ARE HIDING SOMETHING...

MOMENTS LATER...
SPEED! YOUR MOTHER CALLED!

CARL'S BODY IS BEING SHIPPED BACK TO GEORGIA TOMORROW! SHE GAVE ME THE ADRESS OF THE FUNERAL HOME, SO YOU CAN PAY YOUR RE-SPECTS THIS EVENING!

I-I DON'T KNOW, TRIXIE! I'M NOT SURE I CAN TAKE SEEING HIM AGAIN! NOT AFTER---

I KNOW IT'LL BE DIFFICULT FOR YOU SPEED--- BUT I'LL BE WITH YOU!
ME, TOO!
THANKS, GUYS!

THAT EVENING...
MAYHER FUNERAL PARLOR
WHY YES, TREASURED MEMENTOES ARE OFTEN INTERNED WITH THE DECEASED!
GOOD! I'D LIKE YOU TO PUT THIS AROUND CARL'S NECK!

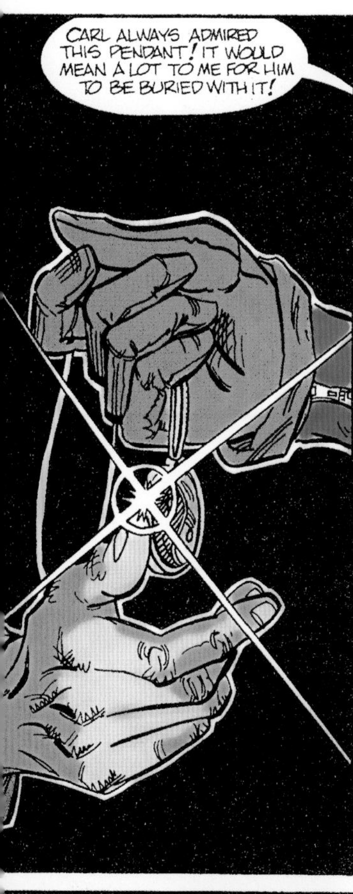
CARL ALWAYS ADMIRED THIS PENDANT! IT WOULD MEAN A LOT TO ME FOR HIM TO BE BURIED WITH IT!

I'D BE HAPPY TO OBLIGE!
BY THE WAY---

DID THE AUTOPSY PINPOINT JUST WHAT KIND OF ANIMAL KILLED CARL?
THE CORONER'S REPORT SAID THAT IT WAS SOME TYPE OF CANUS LUPUS ---A WOLF!

HOW COULD A WOLF HAVE CAUSED THAT MUCH DAMAGE?
I DON'T KNOW-- BUT I'LL BET LOU DOES! HE'S BEEN ACTING AW-FULLY STRANGE! IF I COULD ONLY GET HIM AWAY FROM HIS SISTER!

JUST LEAVE HER TO ME! I'LL SAY I NEED TO TALK WITH HER ABOUT THE NEW RACIN' REGULATIONS---
--THEN I'LL TURN ON THE CHARM! SHE'LL BE BUSY ALL EVENING!

YOU BOTH OUGHT TO BE CAREFUL. LOU PINE SOUNDS AN AWFUL LOT LIKE LUPINE-- AND THAT MEANS "WOLF"!

LATER THAT NIGHT, AT THE HOTEL...
THERE THEY GO! NOW WE CAN TALK TO LOU WITHOUT WORRYING ABOUT HIS SISTER!
I'LL MEET YOU AT LOU'S ROOM, LATER!

THERE'S SOMETHING I HAVE TO GET--- BEFORE IT'S TOO LATE!
WHAT IS IT?

IF WE NEED IT, YOU'LL FIND OUT--- AND IF WE DON'T NEED IT, I'D FEEL SILLY IF I TOLD YOU!

MOMENTS LATER...
WHY AM I SO NERVOUS? I DON'T BELIEVE IN WEREWOLVES!

I'M SURE THERE'S A LOGICAL EXPLANATION FOR THE ATTACK ...AND THAT LOU KNOWS WHAT IT IS!
KNOCK! KNOCK!

SPEED! WHAT ARE YOU DOING HERE? YOU'D BETTER LEAVE, BEFORE SUE--
SHE'S GONE OUT WITH SPARKY FOR THE EVENING! AND I'VE GOT TO TALK TO YOU-- ABOUT CARL'S DEATH!

YOU'VE BEEN ACTING STRANGE EVER SINCE THAT PRACTICE SESSION WE HAD WITH CARL! WHY? WHAT'S WRONG?
I-- I CAN'T TELL YOU! NOW, PLEASE, YOU'VE GOT TO LEAVE!

LOOK! THE FULL MOON IS RISING! GET OUT WHILE YOU STILL CAN!

I'M NOT LEAVING UNTIL I GET SOME ANSWERS!

MAYBE IT'S TIME I QUIT RUNNING FROM THE SECRET THAT'S HAUNTED ME ALL THESE YEARS!
YOU SEE, SPEED EVERY OCTOBER--- WHEN THE FULL MOON RISES--- I BECOME A WOLF. AND I KILL.

MY MOTHER WAS ROMANIAN. ON HALLO-WEEN, WHEN SHE WAS A LITTLE GIRL, SHE WAS BITTEN BY A WOLF! AND EVERY YEAR THEREAFTER..

--DURING OCTOBER'S FULL MOON, SHE BECAME A WOLF! WHEN SHE DIED, THE CURSE PASSED ON TO ME!

THE NIGHT CARL DIED, I WOKE UP COVERED IN BLOOD-- HIS BLOOD! IT HAPPENS EVERY YEAR AT THIS TIME! THE BLACKOUTS, THE KILLINGS---

YOU DIDN'T KILL CARL--AN ANIMAL DID! MAYBE YOU CAUGHT A GLIMPSE OF THE CREATURE, AND YOUR UNCONSCIOUS MIND---

YOU THINK I'M CRAZY?

YOU'RE THE ONE WHO'S CRAZY, IF YOU DON'T LEAVE WHILE YOU STILL CAN!

SUDDENLY...
666
IT DIDN'T TAKE ME LONG TO FIGURE OUT WHAT SPARKY WAS UP TO! YOU THOUGHT YOU WERE CLEVER, SPEED---

---BUT NOW, YOU'RE GOING TO GET MORE THAN YOU BARGAINED FOR!
YOU'VE MADE ME REVEAL MY SECRET TO LOU--- AND FOR THAT, YOU MUST DIE!
NO HE WON'T! THERE WAS ENOUGH TIME FOR THE GUNSMITH TO MAKE TWO SILVER BULLETS-- BUT THEY'LL BE ENOUGH TO STOP YOU!
GRRRRR--- MY TRANSFORMATION STOPPED-- AS SOON AS THE BULLET HIT ME!

GRRR-- STUPID WOMAN! WHAT HAVE YOU DONE? I'M NOT HUMAN---AND I'M NOT WOLF!
UUUGGHH!!
GET AWAY FROM HER!
ALL THESE YEARS... IT'S BEEN SUE! SHE MUST HAVE BEEN DRUGGING ME... AND COVERING ME WITH HER VICTIMS' BLOOD BEFORE I WOKE UP!
LEAVE THEM ALONE!
GRRR--- STAY AWAY! I DON'T WANT TO HURT YOU--BUT, I MUST EAT!
TWISTED MY ANKLE... I'LL NEVER BE ABLE TO REACH THE GUN IN TIME TO STOP HER!

CRASHING THROUGH THE WINDOW... ANOTHER WOLF?
WHERE DID IT COME FROM? IT'S NOT AS EXPERIENCED AT FIGHTING AS MY SISTER... BUT IT'S GIVEN ME THE TIME I NEED...
GRRRRR!!!
KER-CHOW!
...TO DO WHAT HAS TO BE DONE!

I-I'M SORRY SUE! BUT I COULDN'T LET YOU KILL ANY MORE INNOCENT PEOPLE!
AS IF IT KNOWS ITS JOB IS FINISHED, THE MYSTERIOUS WOLF BOUNDS AWAY...
PLEASE, LOU-- FORGIVE ME-- FOR DECEIVING YOU, FOR SO LONG --CHOKE--
OF COURSE, MY DEAR SISTER!

I-I'M STILL SO CONFUSED! THE WOLF THAT SAVED US APPEARED FROM NOWHERE-- AND THEN VANISHED!
LOOK! HERE ON THE FLOOR!

GOOD LORD! IT'S THE PENDANT I LEFT FOR CARL! YOU DON'T SUPPOSE THAT SINCE HE WAS BITTEN BY A WEREWOLF---
I DON'T KNOW WHAT TO THINK! LET'S CALL THE POLICE AND AND GET OUT OF HERE!
NEXT ISSUE: THE ALPHA TEAM RETURNS!

Speed Racer #29

Smith

"IT'S BEEN ALMOST A YEAR ... BUT I'LL NEVER FORGET MY LAST RACE AGAINST THE LEGENDARY COMET CARSON!"
1988 DALLAS RACE OF CHAMPIONS
"I'D TRAILED CARSON THE WHOLE RACE! FINALLY ...ON THE LAST LAP... I WAS IN POSITION TO MAKE MY MOVE."
"SUDDENLY, I WAS IN THE LEAD! UP AHEAD, I SAW THE CHECKERED FLAG WAITING TO SIGNAL MY VICTORY OVER THE DRIVER I HAD IDOLIZED ALL MY LIFE!"
KA BOOM!
"BUT ON THE FINAL TURN, I HEARD TIRES SCREECH BEHIND ME AND I TURNED AROUND TO SEE CARSON'S CAR DISINTEGRATING AGAINST THE WALL!"
BLAZE OF GLORY
LAMAR WALDRON STORY
NORM DWYER PENCILS
JIM BROZMAN INKS
DAN NAKROSIS LETTERS
NOW COMICS STAFF COLORS
MICHELE MACH ART DIRECTOR
KATHERINE LLEWELLYN EDITOR
TONY CAPUTO EDITOR IN CHIEF
NORM DWYER & TAMMY DANIEL COVER ART

AND THE WINNER IS-- SPEED RACER DRIVING THE MACH 5!
"WITHOUT FINISHING MY VICTORY LAP, I SPUN THE CAR AROUND AND HEADED TOWARD THE CRASH SITE!"
SCREE
"I FELT MY HEART POUNDING AS I LEAPT FROM THE MACH 5 TO HELP THE EMERGENCY CREW!"
"CARSON WAS STILL CONSCIOUS AS I HELPED PULL HIM FROM THE WRECKAGE ..."
GET THIS DAD-BLASTED HELMET OFF ME, SO I CAN BREATHE!

THAT'S BETTER COUGH!
SPEED, THAT WAS A REAL FINE MOVE YOU PUT ON ME THERE AT THE END, PARTNER!

I'M SORRY, MR. CARSON! I DIDN'T MEAN TO CAUSE---
YOU DIDN'T CAUSE ANYTHING, SPEED! THAT ACCIDENT WAS MY FAULT!

I WAS JUST A LITTLE TOO ANXIOUS TO GET MY 100TH VICTORY! BUT DON'T YOU WORRY-- COUGH -- I'LL BE BACK RACING BEFORE YOU KNOW IT!

"THEN HE CLOSED HIS EYES AND BECAME AWFULLY STILL...
MR. CARSON!

HURRY!--HE'S LAPSED INTO A COMA!
POOR GUY! EVEN IF HE PULLS THROUGH, HE'LL NEVER WALK AGAIN!
I'M SORRY, SON!

"I STILL REMEMBER WATCHING THE AMBULANCE DRIVE AWAY AND WONDERING IF I'D EVER SEE COMET CARSON AGAIN!"
COME ON, SON-- EVERYONE'S WAITING FOR YOU AT THE WINNER'S CIRCLE!

1989 DALLAS
"NOW, A YEAR LATER, I CAN'T BELIEVE MY EYES! IT'S THE FIRST DAY OF QUALIFYING, AND COMING TOWARD ME IS..."

"...COMET CARSON!"
HOWDY, PARTNERS! BET YOU FOLKS THOUGHT YOU'D SEEN THE LAST OF OL' COMET, EH?
LAST I HEARD, YOU WERE STILL IN A COMA!
WELL, I UP AND GOT BETTER, JUST TO PROVE THOSE DOCTORS WRONG!

IT'S GREAT TO SEE YOU ON YOUR FEET!
MR. CARSON, I---
CALL ME COMET, SON!
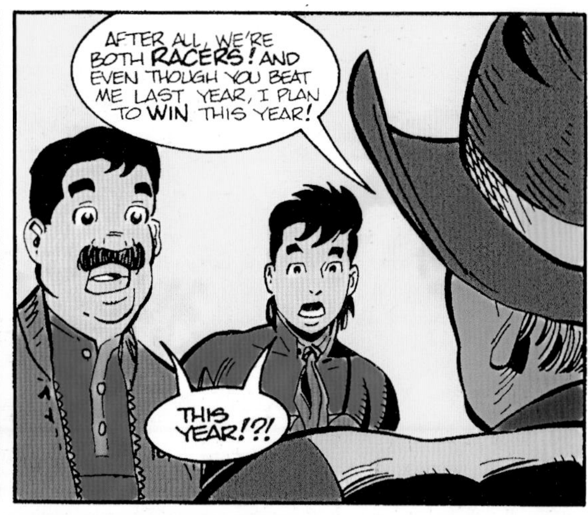
AFTER ALL, WE'RE BOTH RACERS! AND EVEN THOUGH YOU BEAT ME LAST YEAR, I PLAN TO WIN THIS YEAR!
THIS YEAR!?!

I STILL NEED ONE MORE VICTORY-- NUMBER 100-- BEFORE I RE-TIRE! SURE I'VE GOT A LITTLE LIMP, BUT MY REFLEXES ARE AS GOOD AS EVER!

YOU CAN'T BE SERIOUS! WHY, A MAN OF YOUR AGE, COMING OFF SUCH SERIOUS INJURIES-- IT'S IMPOSSIBLE! YOU'D BE CRAZY TO RACE!
Pops

AND HAVEN'T YOU HEARD? ACE DUCEY AND HIS CUT-THROAT ALPHA TEAM HAVE ENTERED! THEY'LL STOP AT NOTHING TO WIN!

LOOK PARTNERS, I'VE BEEN RACING FOR OVER THIRTY YEARS! SURE, I'VE WON BIG RACES AND CHAMPIONSHIPS-- BUT SO HAVE LOTS OF OTHERS!
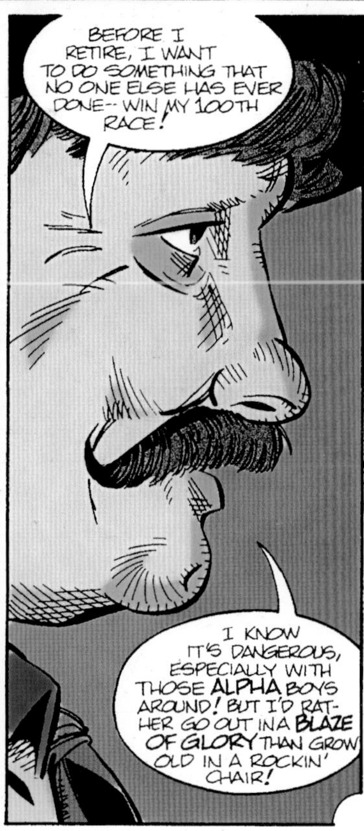
BEFORE I RETIRE, I WANT TO DO SOMETHING THAT NO ONE ELSE HAS EVER DONE-- WIN MY 100TH RACE!
I KNOW IT'S DANGEROUS, ESPECIALLY WITH THOSE ALPHA BOYS AROUND! BUT I'D RAT-HER GO OUT IN A BLAZE OF GLORY THAN GROW OLD IN A ROCKIN' CHAIR!

AN HOUR LATER...
GEE, TRIXIE, I WISH THERE WAS SOME WAY TO KEEP CARSON FROM RACING! HE'S IN NO CONDITION TO RACE!
I KNOW HOW YOU FEEL, SPEED---

--BECAUSE I WISH THERE WAS SOME WAY TO KEEP YOU OUT OF THIS RACE! I DON'T WANT THE ALPHA TEAM GUNNING FOR MY BOYFRIEND!

AND NEXT UP FOR QUALIFY-ING IS SPEED RACER, IN THE MACH 5!

I'VE GOT TO PUT CARSON OUT OF MY MIND AND CONCEN-TRATE ON DRIVING! A GOOD QUALIFYING TIME WILL ENSURE THAT I START WELL AHEAD OF THE ALPHA TEAM!

ALL RIGHT, NUMBER 1, GRAB YOUR WEAPON AND GET INTO POSITION!
YES SIR, ACE!

AND REMEMBER--- JUST ONE SHOT! THIS IS ONLY THE START OF MY PLAN TO AVENGE OUR DEFEAT AT THE HANDS OF SPEED, TWO YEARS AGO!..

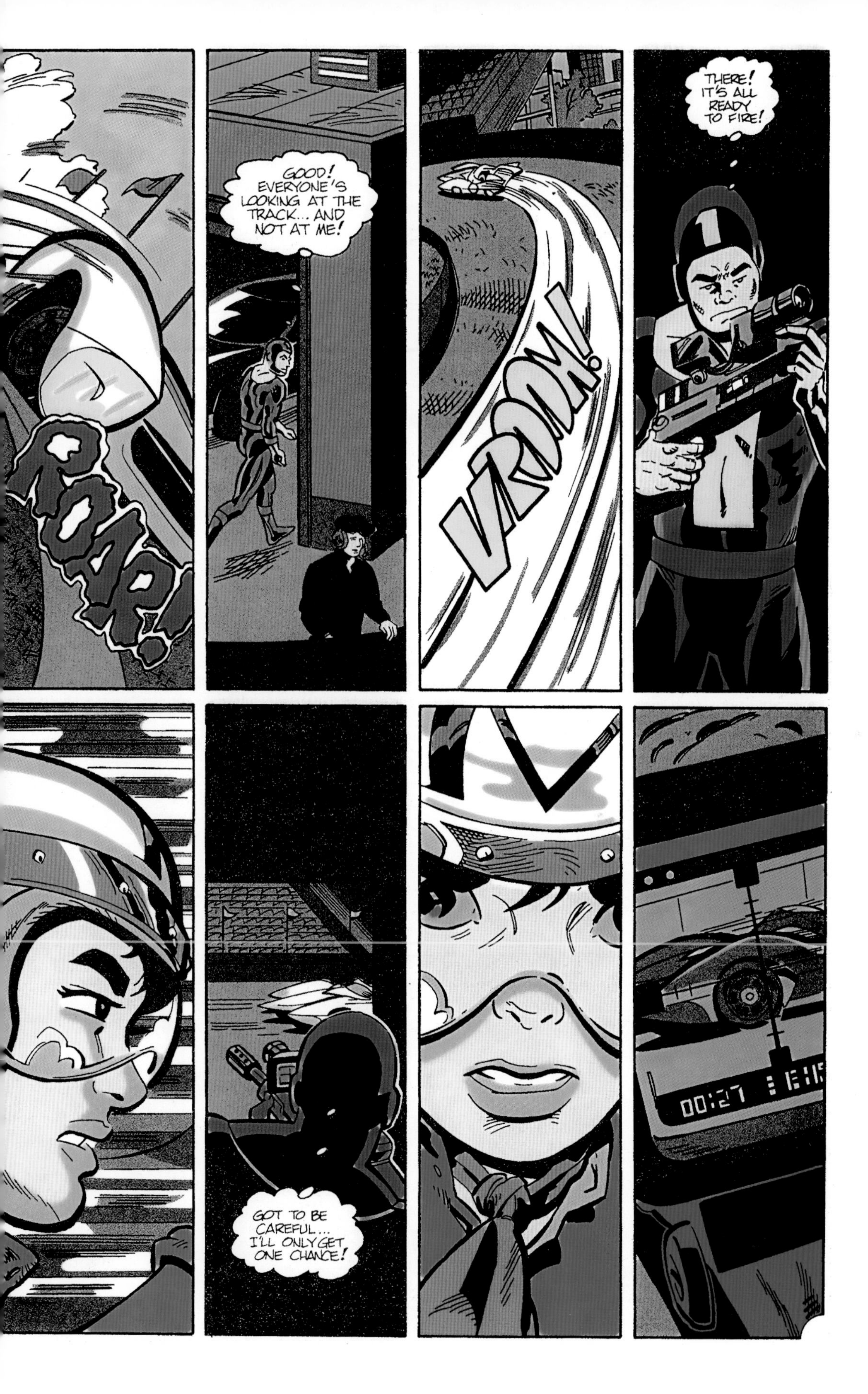
ROAR!
GOOD! EVERYONE'S LOOKING AT THE TRACK... AND NOT AT ME!
VRRROOM!
THERE! IT'S ALL READY TO FIRE!
GOT TO BE CAREFUL... I'LL ONLY GET ONE CHANCE!
00:27

MY TIRE!
BLOP!
I'M SKIDDING OUT OF CONTROL... AT 200 MILES AN HOUR!
OH, NO! THE WALL! IF I HIT THE BRAKES, IT'LL ONLY MAKE THE SKID WORSE!
HAVE TO STRIKE IT AT AN ANGLE...
SCRAAPE!

...AND HOPE I DON'T GO INTO A SPIN WHEN I COME OFF THE WALL!

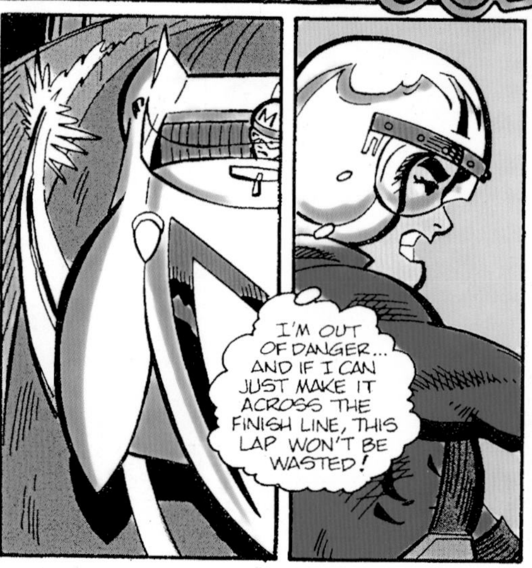
I'M OUT OF DANGER... AND IF I CAN JUST MAKE IT ACROSS THE FINISH LINE, THIS LAP WON'T BE WASTED!

FINISH

ONCE HE CROSSES THE FINISH LINE, SPEED CAREFULLY APPLIES THE BRAKES...
I'VE NEVER HAD A TIRE EXPLODE THE WAY THAT ONE DID! WHAT COULD HAVE CAUSED IT?
SKREEEECH!

SON! ARE YOU ALRIGHT?
I'M FINE-- BUT THERE WAS SOMETHING STRANGE ABOUT THAT BLOW-OUT!

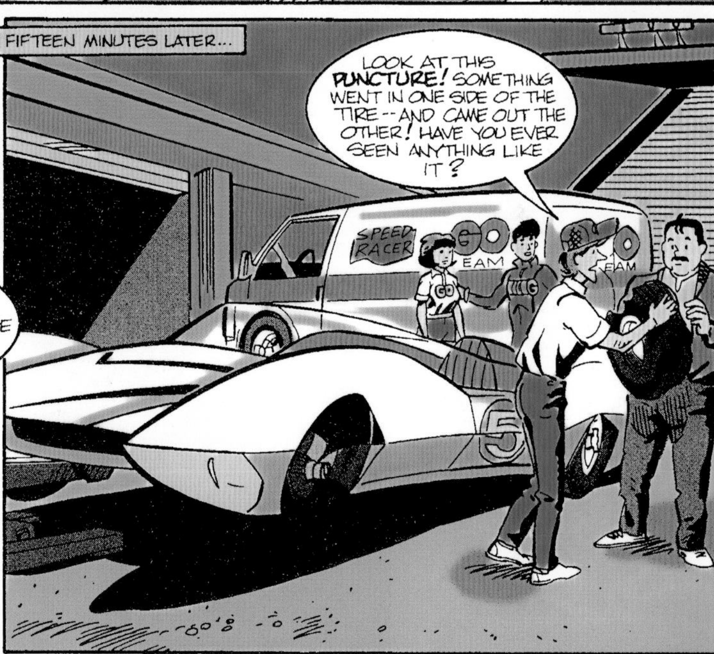
FIFTEEN MINUTES LATER...
LOOK AT THIS PUNCTURE! SOMETHING WENT IN ONE SIDE OF THE TIRE --AND CAME OUT THE OTHER! HAVE YOU EVER SEEN ANYTHING LIKE IT?
SPEED RACER

DURING THE WAR-- WHEN THE GERMANS SHOT THROUGH THE TIRES ON MY JEEP!

IT'S TOO BAD ABOUT YOUR LITTLE ACCIDENT, SPEED... TOO BAD THAT IT WASN'T FATAL! HA! HA! HA! HA!

LATER THAT NIGHT...
THRIFT INN
AW, GEE, POPS-- DO I HAVE TO GO? I'M REALLY TIRED! I'D RATHER STAY HERE AND REST--
GO TEAM

--THAN GO TO SOME BORING MEETING!
I'M SORRY, SON! BUT THIS MEETING IS SO IMPORTANT THAT I WANT EVERYONE THERE! THE FUTURE OF THE GO-TEAM IS AT STAKE!

YOU MAKE IT SOUND SO MYSTERIOUS! CAN'T YOU TELL US ANYTHING MORE?
THAT'S WHAT THE MEETING IS FOR! NOW COME ON, WE'D BETTER GET GOING!

LATER, IN THE FASHIONABLE TURTLE CREEK SECTION OF DALLAS...
GO TEAM

MR. MOORE IS EXPECTING YOU! FOLLOW ME, PLEASE!

PLEASED TO MEET YOU, MR. MOORE! THIS IS QUITE A HOUSE YOU HAVE HERE!
JUST CALL ME SAM! THIS IS JUST MY LITTLE TOWN HOUSE! MY BIG PLACE IS AT THE RANCH, THIRTY MILES NORTH OF HERE!

NOW, COME ON INTO THE DININ' ROOM, SO WE CAN EAT! JUST LET ME KNOW WHAT YOU'D LIKE AND MY CHEF WILL WHIP IT RIGHT UP!

MINUTES LATER...
MY LOBSTER'S PERFECT! HOW'S YOUR FILET MIGNON?
DELICIOUS, TRIXIE! IT'S BEEN SO LONG SINCE I'VE HAD STEAK THAT I FORGOT HOW GOOD IT TASTES!

LOOK, CHIM-CHIM! MR. MOORE EVEN HAS SOMETHING FOR YOU!
CHIMP CHOW

I SURE APPRECIATE YOU FOLKS JOININ' ME FOR DINNER! JUST LET ME KNOW IF THERE'S ANYTHIN' ELSE I CAN DO FOR YOU!

THE MEAL IS FANTASTIC, SIR. BUT, I CAN'T HELP WONDERING WHY YOU'RE BEING SO NICE TO US? ARE YOU A BIG RACING FAN?

YOU MIGHT SAY THAT, SON-- BUT I'M ALSO A BUSINESSMAN! AND I'M AN EXPERT AT TELLING WHEN A BUSINESS ISN'T FULLY REALIZING ITS POTENTIAL!
WHY, THE GO-TEAM COULD GENERATE TEN TIMES AS MUCH MONEY FROM LICENSING AS FROM RACING--
--IF YOU COULD AFFORD TO HIRE A PUBLICIST TO GET ADVERTISERS INTERESTED! AND THAT'S NOT ALL!
THINK HOW MUCH MORE IMPRESSIVE YOUR VICTORIES WOULD BE, IF YOU HAD ENOUGH MONEY TO HIRE A PROFESSIONAL PIT CREW! WHY, WITH ENOUGH MONEY--
--YOU COULD UPDATE THE MACH 5 AND MAKE IT EVEN FASTER! AND WITH BETTER FINANCING, YOU WOULDN'T HAVE TO STAY IN CHEAP MOTELS AND EAT FAST FOOD ALL THE TIME!

YOU CAN HAVE ALL THOSE THINGS --AND MUCH MORE!
ALL YOU NEED IS A PARTNER! A PARTNER LIKE ME, WITH THE MONEY AND THE CONNECTIONS TO MAKE GO-TEAM, INC. THE MOST UP-TO-DATE RACING COMPANY IN THE WORLD!
GO TEAM
HEADQUARTERS
SAN FRANCISCO
IT SOUNDS GREAT!
AND I'M SURE I SPEAK FOR EVERYONE HERE WHEN I SAY THAT WE'D LOVE TO HAVE YOU AS OUR PARTNER!
FINE! WE'LL SIGN THE CONTRACTS TONIGHT... AND I'LL MOVE YOU INTO A BETTER HOTEL IMMEDIATELY! FROM NOW ON, IT'S FIRST CLASS ALL THE WAY FOR GO-TEAM, INC.!

AN HOUR LATER...
WOW! MY PARENTS HAVE STAYED IN SOME PRETTY LAVISH HOTELS --BUT I'LL BET THEY'VE NEVER HAD A SUITE THIS BIG!
THIS HOTEL ROOM IS LARGER THAN OUR HOUSE! IT MUST BE AWFUL-LY EXPENSIVE!
DON'T WORRY! SAM SAYS THAT GO TEAM, INC. IS PAY-ING ALL OF OUR EX-PENSES FROM NOW ON!

I'M WORRIED, TRIXIE! IT ALL SEEMS TOO GOOD TO BE TRUE!
IT'S QUITE A CHANGE, ISN'T IT?
WHY IS SAM GIVING US SO MUCH, NOW? WE HAVEN'T EVEN WON ANY RACES FOR HIM!
MAYBE HE'S ONE OF THOSE TEXAS MILLION-AIRES WITH MORE MONEY THAN HE KNOWS WHAT TO DO WITH!
IT JUST SEEMS FISHY, SOMEHOW! I'M NOT SURE I TRUST HIM!
YOUR FATHER SEEMS TO--- AND HE'S ALWAYS MADE GOOD BUSINESS DECISIONS!
YEAH, BUT HE SEEMS DAZZLED BY SAM'S BIG TALK AND FANCY PLANS. I'M NOT SURE---

LOOK, SPEED, YOU AND YOUR FAMILY HAVE WORKED SO HARD FOR SO LONG! THIS IS YOUR BIG BREAK! RELAX AND ENJOY IT, WHILE YOU CAN!

THE NEXT MORNING...
AREN'T YOU COMING IN, TRIXIE? I STILL HAVE ONE MORE QUALIFYING LAP!
DALLAS MOTOR SPEEDWAY PITS
PLEASE PRESENT YOUR PIT PASS
5
POPS SAID HE DIDN'T NEED ME-- SO I'M GOING TO GET IN A FULL DAY OF SHOPPING BEFORE TOMORROW'S RACE! SEE YOU LATER!

HI, MR. CAR-- ER, I MEAN, COMET! HOW DID THE QUALIFYING GO?
JUST FINE, SPEED!
10

I'LL BE STARTIN' PRETTY FAR BACK IN THE PACK-- BUT I CAN'T TELL YOU HOW GOOD IT FEELS TO KNOW I'LL HAVE A CHANCE TO RACE AGAIN!

IT'S GOING TO---
WHOA! LOOK WHO'S HERE!

SPEED, I'D LIKE YOU TO MEET MY DAUGHTER, LOUISE, AND MY GRANDSON, RANDY!
ARE YOU GOING TO WATCH THE RACE TOMORROW, RANDY?
YOU BET! AND GRANDPA IS GOING TO WIN! HE PROMISED!

MOMENTS LATER, AFTER SPEED EXCUSES HIMSELF.
FATHER, I STILL THINK IT'S TOO DANGEROUS FOR YOU TO---
MY MIND'S MADE UP! IT'S THE ONLY WAY TO PAY FOR RANDY'S OPERATION!

SO THAT'S WHY COMET IS SO DETERMINED TO RACE AGAIN! THAT PUTS ME IN A REALLY AWKWARD POSITION!
POPS SAYS THE NEW COMPANY NEEDS A WIN TO GET OFF TO A GOOD START ... BUT I'D HATE TO KEEP LITTLE RANDY FROM GETTING HIS OPERATION!

WHAT ARE ALL THOSE PEOPLE DOING AROUND THE MACH 5? IS THAT OUR NEW PIT CREW?

WHAT'S WRONG, SPARKY?
EVER SINCE THESE GUYS SHOWED UP, I HAVEN'T HAD ANYTHING TO DO!

HI, SON! LOOK AT THIS PIT CREW! AREN'T THEY GREAT?
YOU'D BETTER GET READY-- IT'S TIME FOR YOUR FINAL QUALIFYING LAP! AND AFTER WHAT HAPPENED YESTERDAY, WE NEED A GOOD ONE!

MINUTES LATER...
HEY, BOSS, DO YOU WANT ME TO GET THE GUN READY?
NO! IT WOULD BE TOO RISKY TO TRY THE SAME STUNT, AGAIN!

SAY, DID YOU SEE THE GO-TEAMS NEW PIT CREW? THEY'RE A CRACKERJACK BUNCH! IT'S GOING TO MAKE OUR JOB EVEN TOUGHER!
BAH! ALL THE PIT CREWS IN THE WORLD COULDN'T KEEP ME FROM GETTING RE-VENGE ON SPEED!

WE'RE GOING TO USE THE SQUEEZE PLAY MANEUVER THAT WAS SO SUCCESSFUL IN MONTE CARLO, LAST YEAR! THE THREE OF US WILL GANG UP ON THE OTHER CARS---

---ONE AT A TIME, SAVING SPEED UNTIL LAST! THEN, WITH NO OTHER CARS LEFT ON THE TRACK TO STOP US, WE'LL MAKE SURE THAT SPEED HAS A FATAL ACCIDENT!

THE FOLLOWING DAY, AS THE RACE GETS UNDERWAY...
TO WIN THIS RACE, I'LL HAVE TO STAY AS FAR AHEAD OF THE ALPHA TEAM AS POSSIBLE!
PACE CAR

I JUST HOPE COMET KEEPS OUT OF THEIR WAY! I'D HATE TO SEE ANYTHING HAPPEN TO HIM!

THAT'S STRANGE... THE ALPHA TEAM IS SLOWING DOWN, LETTING CARS PASS THEM!
PACE CAR

THIS IS ACE CALLING NUMBER ONE AND NUMBER EIGHT! COMMENCE MANEUVER!

WITHIN SECONDS, THEIR FIRST VICTIM IS SURROUNDED AND FORCED INTO THE WALL ON A DANGEROUS TURN...

KA-BOOM!

THOSE MONSTERS! THEY DELIBERATELY CAUSED THAT CRASH!

THAT WAS AN EXCELLENT MOVE! NOTHING LIKE A LITTLE VARIETY TO SPICE UP A RACE!

ONE BY ONE, THE OTHER CARS ARE FORCED OFF THE TRACK BY THE ALPHA TEAM...
UNTIL...

ONLY ONE MORE LAP TO GO...BUT THERE ARE JUST FIVE CARS LEFT IN THE RACE! COMET, MYSELF... AND THE ALPHA TEAM!

OH, NO! THEY'VE SURROUNDED COMET.

I'VE GOT TO HIT THE BRAKES SLOWLY...

...AND HOPE THAT ACE DOESN'T CRASH INTO ME!

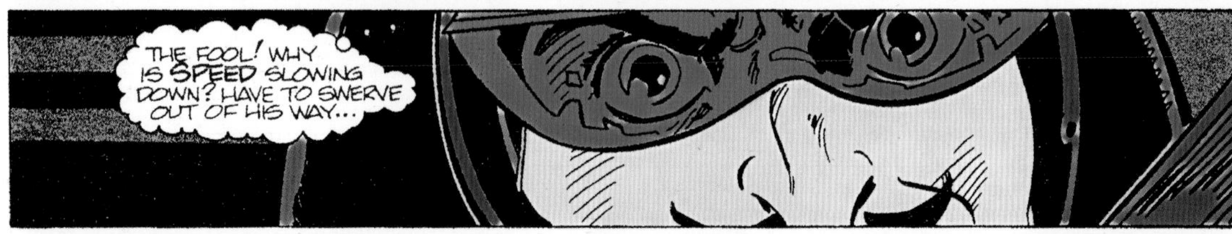
THE FOOL! WHY IS SPEED SLOWING DOWN? HAVE TO SWERVE OUT OF HIS WAY...

KRASH
BLAST IT! SPEED MADE ME CRASH INTO MY OWN TEAMMATE!

I'VE GOT TO CLEAR OUT OF CARSON'S WAY, SO HE CAN GET AWAY FROM THE OTHER DRIVER...

AND MY **ION JACKS** SHOULD DO THE TRICK!

THE JACKS PROPEL THE **MACH 5** HIGH INTO THE AIR, ALLOWING CARSON TO PASS SAFELY UNDERNEATH

GET ON THE RADIO! TELL **NUMBER 8** TO FORGET ABOUT TRYING TO WIN THE RACE--
--I WANT HIM TO STOP SPEED AT ANY COST!

IF CARSON DOESN'T WIN THIS RACE, HE'LL KEEP ENTERING UNTIL HE DOES-- AND I MIGHT NOT BE AROUND TO SAVE HIM!
I'VE MADE UP MY MIND... POPS WILL HAVE TO BE SATISFIED WITH **SECOND PLACE** THIS TIME!

SUDDENLY...
IS THIS GUY **CRAZY**? HE'S GOING TO KILL US BOTH!

RACE
AND THE WINNER IS-- COMET CARSON! HE BECOMES THE FIRST RACER TO WIN ONE HUNDRED CHAMPIONSHIP RACES!
11

OH NO! SPEED HASN'T CROSSED THE FINISH LINE! WE WON'T GET ANY PRIZE MONEY--
FORGET THE PRIZE MONEY-- I JUST HOPE SPEED WASN'T INJURED!
GO

ARE YOU ALL RIGHT?
JUST A LITTLE SHAKEN UP!
BUT WHY DID YOU GIVE UP THE LEAD? YOU COULD HAVE WON!

11
SOME THINGS MEAN MORE THAN WINNING, POPS!
THAT'S GOOD PHILOSOPHY--
--BUT IT DOESN'T PAY THE BILLS! REMEMBER THAT NEXT TIME!

THERE WON'T BE A NEXT TIME! OUR CONTRACT GIVES ME FINAL AUTHORITY--
--AND BECAUSE YOU LOST, I'M TAKING POSSESSION OF THE MACH 5, NOW!
END

Speed Racer #30

SPEED RACER™
IT'S A RACERS' LIFE
LAMAR WALDRON WRITER
NORM DWYER PENCILS
BRIAN THOMAS INKS
PATRICK WILLIAMS • LETTERS
JOSEPH ALLEN • COLORS
KATHERINE LLEWELLYN • EDITOR
MICHELE MACH • ART DIRECTOR
TONY CAPUTO • EDITOR IN CHIEF
COVER BY NORM DWYER AND TAMMY DANIEL
I'M THE PRESIDENT OF GO-TEAM, INC. AND I'M TAKING THE MACH 5! I SHOULD HAVE KNOWN BETTER THAN TO GO INTO BUSINESS WITH A BUNCH OF LOSERS!
YOU CAN'T TAKE THAT CAR! I DESIGNED IT! I BUILT IT! AND NO ONE BUT MY SON, SPEED, IS GOING TO DRIVE IT!
I THOUGHT YOU WERE MY FRIEND, SAM-- BUT NOW I KNOW WHAT A SNAKE YOU REALLY ARE. OUR PARTNERSHIP IS OVER!

WHAT PARTNERSHIP? ACCORDING TO THE FINE PRINT IN THE CONTRACT YOU SIGNED, I OWN **GO-TEAM, INC.**--
CONTRACT
AND YOU'RE JUST AN **EMPLOYEE!**

WHAT!? YOU NEVER TOLD ME THAT!

OF COURSE NOT, YOU STUPID OAF! IF I HAD, YOU'D NEVER HAVE SIGNED OVER THE **MACH 5** TO THE CORPORATION!

ALL YOUR BIG **PLANS** ABOUT CONSTRUCTING A GO-TEAM BUILDING, ALL THE MONEY WE WERE GOING TO MAKE-- THEY WERE ALL **LIES!**

ACCORDING TO THE LAW, WHAT **I SAY** DOESN'T MATTER-- ONLY WHAT'S **WRITTEN DOWN!** AND OUR **CONTRACT** STATES THAT THE **MACH 5** IS **MINE!**

POPS! PLEASE-- TRY TO RELAX! REMEMBER WHAT THE DOCTOR SAID ABOUT TOO MUCH **STRESS!**
I WON'T LET THIS **CROOK** STEAL MY **LIFE'S WORK,** SON, I'LL--

* CARDIO-PULMONARY RESUSCITATION

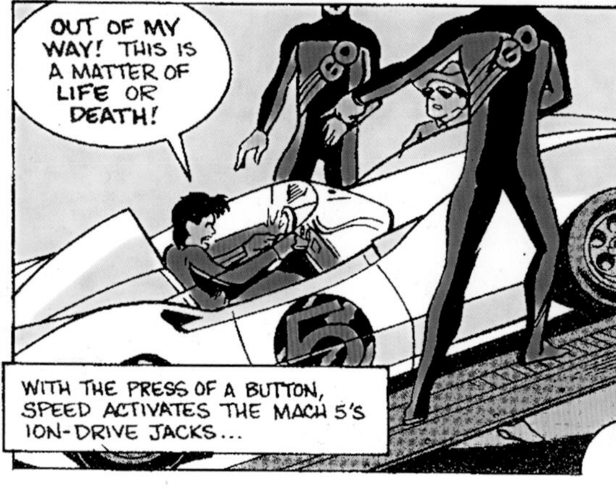

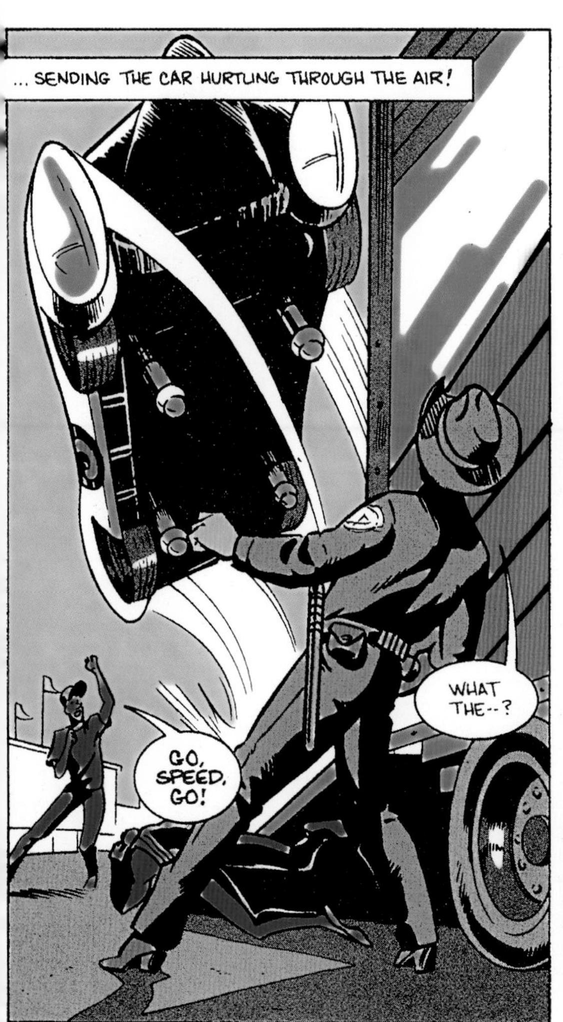
... SENDING THE CAR HURTLING THROUGH THE AIR!
GO, SPEED, GO!
WHAT THE--?

NOW HOLD ON, YOUNG FELLA!

HE'S STEALING MY PROPERTY! ARREST HIM, IMMEDIATELY!

LOOK, SON-- MY DEPUTY IS CALLING AN AMBULANCE FOR YOUR FATHER!
SHERIFF

GET OUT OF MY WAY!
BUT THAT CAR BELONGS TO MR. MOORE, NOW--AND I CAN'T LET YOU TAKE IT!
SNAP!

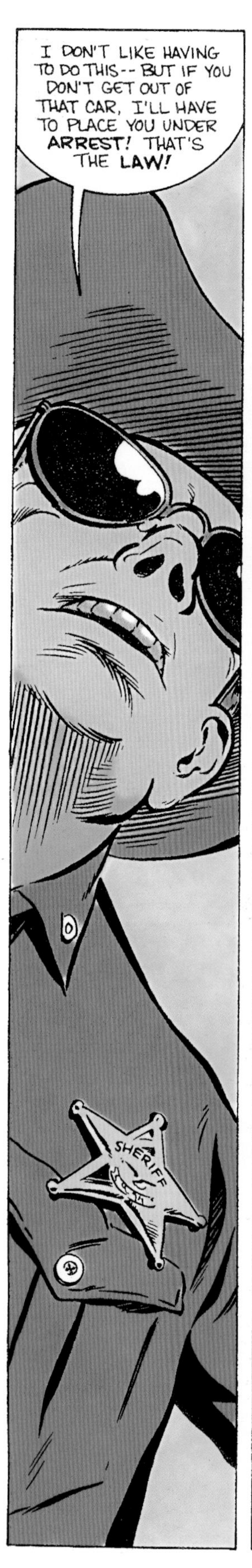
I DON'T LIKE HAVING TO DO THIS-- BUT IF YOU DON'T GET OUT OF THAT CAR, I'LL HAVE TO PLACE YOU UNDER **ARREST!** THAT'S THE **LAW!**
SHERIFF

MY FATHER'S **LIFE** IS AT STAKE! I WON'T LET HIM **DIE!**

SHERIFF
WE'RE DOIN' OUR BEST TO MAKE SURE THAT DOESN'T HAPPEN!
A CARDIAC EMERGENCY TEAM WILL BE HERE IN MINUTES, AND YOUR MOTHER IS DOING C.P.R.!

I KNOW IT'S HARD FOR YOU TO ACCEPT, BUT THERE'S NOTHING MORE YOU CAN DO-- EXCEPT GET THROWN IN **JAIL**, IF YOU DON'T GET OUT OF MR. MOORE'S CAR **RIGHT NOW!**

Y-YOU'RE RIGHT! I CAN'T HELP MY FAMILY FROM A JAIL CELL!

AS FOR YOU- I'M GOING TO MAKE YOU PAY FOR WHAT YOU'VE DONE TO POPS IF IT'S THE LAST THING I DO!
AMBULANCE

I DON'T CARE WHAT THE LAW SAYS-- YOU'RE A LIAR, AND A CHEAT, AND A THIEF! AND IF MY FATHER DIES--

THAT WOULD BE A SHAME-- BECAUSE HE WOULDN'T GET TO SEE HOW MUCH HIS FAMILY IS GOING TO SUFFER! YOU SEE, SPEED, THAT CONTRACT YOUR FATHER SIGNED--

--TURNED OVER CONTROL OF ALL OF YOUR FAMILY'S PERSONAL PROPERTY TO THE CORPORATION! I TOLD HIM IT WAS FOR TAX REASONS--AND THE FOOL BELIEVED ME!
EVERYTHING-- THE VAN, YOUR RACING TROPHIES, EVEN YOUR HOME-- BELONGS TO ME!
HA! HA! HA!

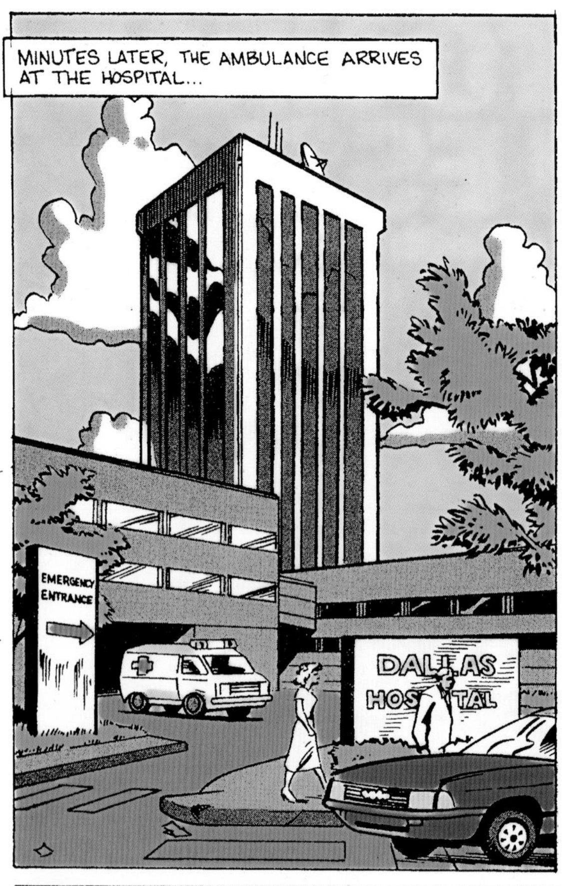
MINUTES LATER, THE AMBULANCE ARRIVES AT THE HOSPITAL...
EMERGENCY ENTRANCE
DALLAS HOSPITAL

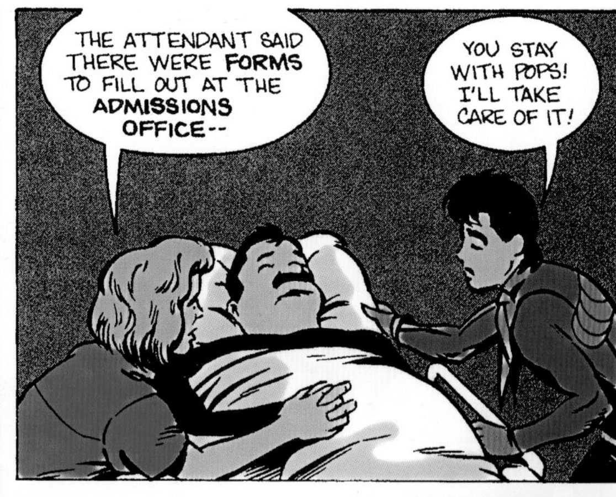
THE ATTENDANT SAID THERE WERE FORMS TO FILL OUT AT THE ADMISSIONS OFFICE--
YOU STAY WITH POPS! I'LL TAKE CARE OF IT!

SPARKY--CAN YOU KEEP AN EYE ON SPRIDLE WHILE TRIXIE AND I GO TO ADMISSIONS?
SURE, SPEED!

MOMENTS LATER...
ADMISSIONS
EXCUSE ME, MA'AM, BUT THIS FORM SAYS WE HAVE TO HAVE INSURANCE OR PAY CASH IN ADVANCE!
POPS CANCELLED HIS OLD POLICY LAST WEEK, AND WE'RE LOW ON MONEY--
ADMISSIONS

THEN WE WON'T BE ABLE TO ADMIT HIM!
HE'LL BE RELEASED AS SOON AS HE'S STABILIZED!

DON'T YOU UNDERSTAND? HE'S HAD A HEART ATTACK! HE NEEDS MEDICAL SUPERVISION!
THIS ISN'T A CHARITY HOSPITAL!
WHO'S GOING TO PAY?

HERE! THIS SHOULD TAKE CARE OF EVERYTHING--I HAVE A $50,000 CREDIT LIMIT!
AMERICAN EXCESS GOLD CARD
FINE! THAT SHOULD COVER THINGS FOR A FEW DAYS--
MAYBE EVEN A WEEK!

LATER THAT NIGHT...

UH?
WHY, IT'S--

ACE DEUCEY, AT YOUR SERVICE. I HEARD WHAT HAPPENED TO YOUR OLD MAN--
--AND FIGURED YOU MIGHT BE LOOKING FOR A JOB! THE ALPHA TEAM--

--IS ALWAYS LOOKING FOR GOOD RACERS, WHO ARE WILLING TO DO ANYTHING TO WIN! I COULD TEACH YOU ENOUGH TRICKS TO--

GET OUT OF HERE, ACE-- BEFORE I THROW YOU OUT!

KEEP THIS!
YOU MIGHT CHANGE YOUR MIND--
ACE
DEUCEY

--WHEN YOU AND YOUR FAMILY GET HUNGRY ENOUGH!
ACE
DEUCEY

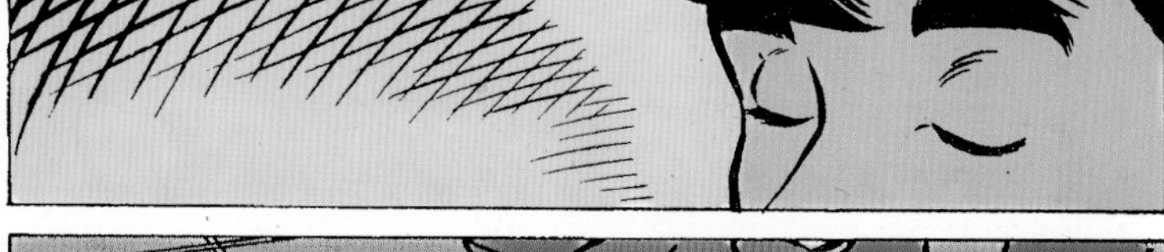

MEANWHILE, BACK AT SAM'S MANSION...
AS SOON AS I GET THOSE DENTS FIXED, THE MACH 5 WILL BE THE PRIDE OF MY COLLECTION!
EXCUSE ME, SIR! MR. DILLIN IS ON THE PHONE!

YES, MR. DILLIN-- EVERYTHING WORKED OUT EXACTLY AS YOU PLANNED! THE OLD MAN IS IN THE HOSPITAL AND THE MACH 5 IS OURS!

GOOD! GOOD! THAT YOUNG FOOL, SPEED, WILL LIVE TO RUE THE DAY HE TRIED TO TOPPLE MY DRUG EMPIRE!

YOU SHOULD HAVE SEEN SPEED'S FACE WHEN HIS FATHER KEELED OVER! IT ALMOST MADE UP FOR ALL THE MONEY I LOST WHEN HIS MEDDLING RUINED OUR BUSINESS DEAL!

DON'T WORRY, SAM! I MAY BE IN PRISON, BUT MY MILLIONS CAN STILL MAKE IT WELL WORTH YOUR WHILE TO HELP ME ACHIEVE MY REVENGE!

WE'VE ONLY JUST BEGUN TO MAKE SPEED SUFFER!
HERE'S WHAT I WANT YOU TO DO NEXT! CALL OUR REAL ESTATE ATTORNEYS IN SAN FRANCISCO AND HAVE THEM--

THE FOLLOWING WEEK, IN SAN FRANCISCO...
SAN FRANCISCO
THANKS SO MUCH FOR HAVING POPS FLOWN HOME, TRIXIE!
NOW THAT POPS IS HERE,
HE CAN STAY AT THE COUNTY HOSPITAL FOR FREE!
I JUST WISH MY CREDIT LIMIT WASN'T EXHAUSTED, SO I COULD CONTINUE TO HELP!

I NEVER TOLD YOU, TRIXIE-- BUT I'VE ALWAYS THOUGHT YOU'D MAKE A WONDERFUL DAUGHTER-IN-LAW, SOMEDAY!
ONE CRISIS AT A TIME, ALL RIGHT?
SAN FRANCISCO PUBLIC HOSPITAL

HEY--WHAT MAKES YOU THINK I'D EVEN WANT TO MARRY YOU?
I CAN DREAM, CAN'T I?

YOU TWO WILL HAVE PLENTY OF TIME TO PLAN YOUR FUTURE AFTER WE GET POPS BACK ON HIS FEET AND SPEED BACK ON THE TRACK!

I'M SORRY IF I SOUNDED GLIB ABOUT THAT MARRIAGE STUFF! I REALLY APPRECIATE ALL YOU'VE DONE, TRIXIE!

I WISH YOU DIDN'T HAVE TO LEAVE SO SOON!
ME TOO-- BUT MY FLIGHT TO **NEW GUINEA** TAKES OFF IN JUST A FEW MINUTES! IT TOOK THE LAST OF MY MONEY--

--BUT IF I CAN CATCH UP TO MY **PARENTS'** EXPEDITION, I'M SURE THEY'LL HELP YOU GET THE MACH 5 BACK! IT'S THE ONLY WAY!

I KNOW! BUT I JUST-- WELL, I'M REALLY GOING TO MISS YOU AND-- AND--

AND?

BE CAREFUL!
DON'T WORRY ABOUT ME-- JUST TAKE GOOD CARE OF POPS!

LATER, IN INTENSIVE CARE...
ARE WE STILL IN TEXAS? SORRY-- CAN'T REMEMBER MUCH--THE MEDICATION KEEPS ME SO GROGGY!
YOU'RE BACK HOME IN SAN FRANCISCO! THE FOLKS HERE AT COUNTY HOSPITAL ARE TAKING GOOD CARE OF YOU!
HOW DID WE DO IN THE RACE, SON? DID WE WIN?
ER, UH--
I'M AFRAID THAT VISITING HOURS ARE OVER, SO WE'LL HAVE TO TALK ABOUT THAT LATER! GET PLENTY OF SLEEP, ALL RIGHT, DEAR?
I TRIED TO CALL HOME TO SEE IF SPARKY AND SPRIDLE ARE BACK WITH THE VAN, BUT THE OPERATOR SAID IT HAD BEEN DISCONNECTED!
THAT'S ODD! OH WELL, YOU'D BETTER TAKE A CAB AND HEAD RIGHT OVER-- SPRIDLE AND CHIM-CHIM ARE PROBABLY DRIVING SPARKY CRAZY!
IT LOOKS LIKE I'M A LITTLE LOW ON MONEY, SON! WOULD YOU MIND TAKING THE SUBWAY?
WITH ALL THE TROUBLE I'VE BEEN THROUGH, IT FEELS GREAT TO BE BACK IN SAN FRANCISCO!
I CAN'T WAIT TO GET HOME!
SAN FRANCISCO PUBLIC HOSPITAL

BUT TWO HOURS LATER, WHEN SPEED FINALLY ARRIVES HOME...
WHAT HAPPENED TO OUR HOUSE?

SPARKY, WHO DID THIS?
SPEED RACER
SAM'S MEN! THEY WERE FINISHING JUST AS WE DROVE UP! I TRIED TO STOP THEM--

--BUT THE SHERIFF WAS WITH THEM! HE SAID IT WAS ALL LEGAL!
I CAN'T BELIEVE IT!
WE'VE BEEN LOCKED OUT OF OUR OWN HOUSE!

WHY CAN'T I GO TO MY ROOM? sniff
DON'T CRY, SPRIDLE! IT-- IT'S GOING TO BE OKAY!

REX

THE LAST PICTURE TAKEN OF MY BROTHER, REX--
--AND THEY SMASHED IT! sniff THOSE--THOSE--

--THOSE **MONSTERS!** I DON'T KNOW WHY THEY'RE PUTTING US THROUGH **HELL,** BUT I'M **NOT** GOING TO LET THEM **DESTROY** MY **FAMILY!**

SPARKY, HELP ME LOAD ALL THE ESSENTIALS INTO THE VAN! I'LL ASK OUR NEIGHBORS IF THEY CAN STORE THE REST!
RIGHT, SPEED!

SPRIDLE, POPS IS STILL SICK! YOU AND I HAVE TO TAKE HIS PLACE FOR A WHILE, AND HELP MOM OUT! IT WON'T BE EASY, BUT--
YOU CAN COUNT ON ME, BIG BROTHER!

LATER THAT EVENING, BACK AT THE HOSPITAL...
MOM, I'M AFRAID I'VE GOT SOME BAD NEWS! YOU'D BETTER SIT DOWN!
I'VE BEEN SITTING FOR HOURS! BESIDES, AFTER ALL WE'VE BEEN THROUGH, WHAT COULD BE SO BAD?

AFTER SPEED FINISHES HIS EXPLANATION...
THEY CAN'T JUST TAKE OUR HOUSE! I'LL FIND AN ATTORNEY AND FIGHT THEM IN COURT!

SURE, MOM--BUT IN THE MEANTIME, WHERE CAN WE STAY?
I'M THE **HOSPITAL SOCIAL WORKER**--AND I COULDN'T HELP OVERHEARING YOUR PROBLEM! I HAVE A SUGGESTION--

MEANWHILE, AT SAM MOORE'S ESTATE IN DALLAS...
VROOM

MAN, THIS IS A GREAT CAR!

SUDDENLY...
CHOKE
SP-UT-TER

IT'S CHOKING DOWN! WHAT'S WRONG WITH IT?

BACK AT SAM'S GARAGE...
SORRY, SIR, BUT I JUST CAN'T FIGURE OUT HOW TO FIX IT! I'VE NEVER SEEN ANOTHER CAR LIKE IT!
BLAST IT! WHAT GOOD IS IT, IF IT WON'T RUN?

MINUTES LATER...
WHAT'S THAT, DILLIN? AUCTION IT OFF? BUT IT DOESN'T WORK!

THAT DOESN'T MATTER! IT'S STILL THE MOST FAMOUS CAR IN THE WORLD! WE'LL GET A FORTUNE FOR IT!

THAT NIGHT, BACK IN SAN FRANCISCO...
DON'T FEEL BAD, MOM! LOTS OF FAMILIES HAVE TO STAY IN HOMELESS SHELTERS, SOMETIMES! IT'S NOTHING TO BE ASHAMED OF!
I JUST FEEL LIKE I'VE LET YOU ALL DOWN!

WAIT A MINUTE! I THOUGHT I HEARD SOMEONE ON TV MENTION THE MACH 5!

CROTHEBY'S AUCTION GALLERY IN NEW YORK SAYS THAT FRIDAY'S SALE OF THE MACH 5 RACE CAR--
IT IS THE MACH 5!

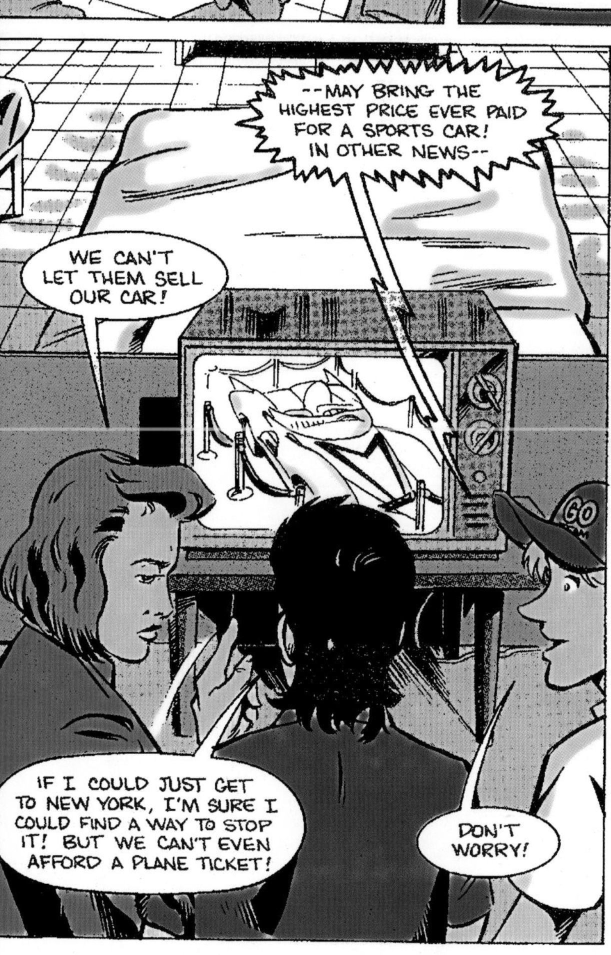
--MAY BRING THE HIGHEST PRICE EVER PAID FOR A SPORTS CAR! IN OTHER NEWS--
WE CAN'T LET THEM SELL OUR CAR!
IF I COULD JUST GET TO NEW YORK, I'M SURE I COULD FIND A WAY TO STOP IT! BUT WE CAN'T EVEN AFFORD A PLANE TICKET!
DON'T WORRY!

HERE'S THE ANSWER TO YOUR PRAYERS! THEY NEED DRIVERS TO DELIVER CARS FROM SAN FRANCISCO TO NEW YORK CITY!
CLASSIFIED ADS
HELP WANTED
BUS DRIVER
COAST TO COAST DRIVERS WANTED
CHAUFFEUR
HELP WANTED
WAITRESS
COOK
WAITER

THE FOLLOWING DAY...
GEE, SPEED-- THE CAR THEY GAVE YOU TO DRIVE TO NEW YORK LOOKS AWFULLY OLD!
ARE YOU SURE IT'LL MAKE IT? MAYBE YOU SHOULD TAKE A GOOD MECHANIC ALONG--
SORRY, SPARKY! BUT I'M DEPENDING ON YOU TO HELP MOM, WHILE I'M GONE!
7145

I'LL DO MY BEST! AND GOOD LUCK IN THE BIG APPLE!
THANKS, OLD PAL-- I'LL NEED ALL THE LUCK I CAN GET! THE AUCTION'S ONLY THREE DAYS AWAY!

POOR SPEED... EVEN IF THAT CLUNKER GETS HIM TO NEW YORK ON TIME, HE DOESN'T STAND A CHANCE! BUT I HAVE TO ADMIRE HIM FOR TRYING!
GO
TEAM

THE HOURS GO BY SLOWLY, AS SPEED PUSHES EASTWARD.
EVERY MILE BRINGS HIM CLOSER TO HIS GOAL...
... AND CLOSER TO COMPLETE EXHAUSTION!

THREE DAYS LATER IN NEW YORK CITY, AFTER SPEED HAS SAFELY DELIVERED THE CAR...
CROTHEBY
5th AVE
MACHY AUCTION TODAY
SO FAR, SO GOOD! ONCE I EXPLAINED WHO I WAS, MR. CROTHEBY HIMSELF AGREED TO SEE ME! I'M SURE I CAN CONVINCE HIM TO STOP THE AUCTION!
86012
PLEASE BE BRIEF! MR. CROTHEBY CAN ONLY SPARE A FEW MINUTES FROM HIS BUSY SCHEDULE!
WHAT CAN I HELP YOU WITH, MY BOY?
THE AUCTION, IT HAS TO BE STOPPED!
AFTER SPEED EXPLAINS HOW HIS FAMILY WAS CHEATED OUT OF THE MACH 5...
AND THAT'S WHY YOU'RE OUR ONLY HOPE!
HMMM-- I SEE!
I'D LIKE TO HELP YOU--BUT MR. MOORE'S COMPANY HAS LEGAL TITLE TO THE CAR, AND A SIGNED CONTRACT FROM OUR FIRM TO CONDUCT THE AUCTION!
THERE'S NOTHING I CAN DO! NOW, IF YOU'LL EX-CUSE ME--
NO! YOU CAN'T SELL THE MACH 5! DON'T YOU UNDERSTAND?
GET YOUR HANDS OFF ME! YOU'VE GOT TO STOP THE AUCTION!

MOMENTS LATER...
I SHOULDN'T HAVE BLOWN MY TOP LIKE THAT! THERE'S NOT MUCH TIME... WHAT CAN I DO NOW?

MAYBE I CAN FIND A LAWYER WILLING TO HELP ME GET AN INJUNCTION TO STOP THE SALE!

WHO AM I KIDDING? I DON'T KNOW ANYONE IN THIS TOWN...
...AND HIRING AN ATTORNEY TAKES REAL MONEY, NOT JUST POCKET CHANGE!

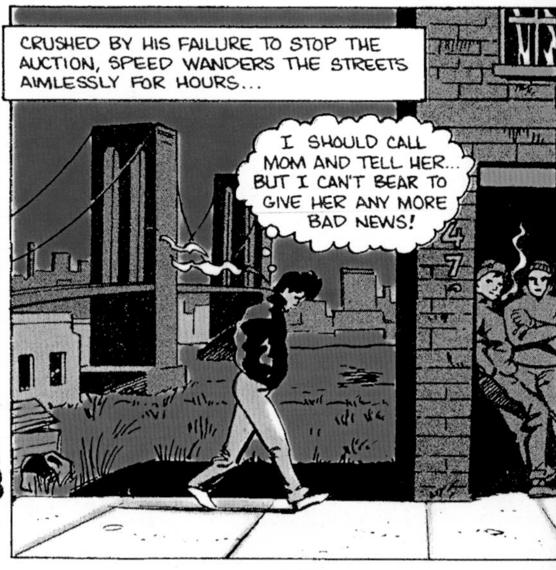
CRUSHED BY HIS FAILURE TO STOP THE AUCTION, SPEED WANDERS THE STREETS AIMLESSLY FOR HOURS...
I SHOULD CALL MOM AND TELL HER... BUT I CAN'T BEAR TO GIVE HER ANY MORE BAD NEWS!

QUICK! GRAB HIS WALLET!
UUUGGHH!!!

BOY, CAN YOU PICK 'EM! HE DIDN'T EVEN HAVE ANY CASH!
C'MON! LET'S GET OUT OF HERE!

MEANWHILE, BACK IN SAN FRANCISCO...
CROTHEBY'S
--AND WE'LL BRING YOU A LIVE REPORT FROM CROTHEBY'S MACH 5 AUCTION AT THE TOP OF THE HOUR!
SPEED MUST NOT HAVE BEEN ABLE TO STOP THE AUCTION! *sniff* BUT WHY HASN'T HE CALLED? I HOPE HE'S ALL RIGHT-- *sob*
SPEED CAN TAKE CARE OF HIMSELF!
RAD

sob I'M SORRY, SPARKY--I'VE TRIED NOT TO CRY DURING THIS WHOLE ORDEAL--BUT IT'S JUST TOO MUCH!
I CAN'T TAKE IT ANY MORE! *sob*
EXCUSE ME, MA'AM!

COMET CARSON!
SPEED LOST THAT RACE--AND GOT INTO ALL THIS TROUBLE--BECAUSE HE WUZ HELPIN' ME OUT!
I HAD SOME PRIZE MONEY LEFT, AFTER PAYIN' MY GRANDSON'S MEDICAL BILLS! IT AIN'T MUCH--BUT I WANTED YOU FOLKS TO HAVE IT!

OH, COMET, THANK YOU! THIS IS THE FIRST GOOD NEWS I'VE HAD IN WEEKS!
RADIOLOGY
EXPRESS PACKAGE FOR MRS. RACER! IT'S INSURED FOR PLENTY, SO YOU'LL NEED TO SIGN FOR IT!

I DON'T BELIEVE IT! IT'S A CHECK FOR $50,000 FROM SPEED'S RACING BUDDY, PAUL TRUMAN*
HIS LETTER SAYS THAT HE'S STILL ON LOCATION--BUT HE READ ABOUT POPS IN RACING WEEKLY AND FIGURED WE MIGHT NEED HELP!
* SEE SPEED RACER #26

I'VE GOT AN OVERNIGHT PACKAGE FOR SPEED RACER. IS HE HERE?
THANKS TO OUR FRIENDS, WE CAN PAY OUR BILLS AND HIRE LEGAL HELP TO FIGHT SAM MOORE THROUGH THE COURTS!
AFTER MOM IDENTIFIES HERSELF AND EXPLAINS THE SITUATION...
IT'S FROM JAPAN!
THE NOTE FROM MR. TETSUI* SAYS THAT LAVISH GIFTS ARE CUSTOMARY IN JAPAN. HE SAYS THAT IN GRATITUDE FOR SPEED'S HELP DEFEATING THE NINJA SABOTEURS--
--HE BEGS HIM TO ACCEPT HIS HUMBLE GIFT OF $100,000!
*SEE SPEED RACER #12
MRS. RACER? I'M FROM THE FIRM OF PEABODY, PEABODY AND SMITH. WE REPRESENT MRS. ALCOTT'S* BUSINESS INTERESTS!
OH YES! THE WOMAN WITH HER OWN ISLAND!
WE REPORT MAINLAND NEWS TO HER, AND WHEN SHE HEARD OF YOUR DIFFICULTIES--
* SEE SPEED RACER # 27
--SHE INSTRUCTED ME TO OFFER ANY FINANCIAL AND LEGAL ASSISTANCE THAT YOU MIGHT REQUIRE!
PARDON ME, BUT THERE'S A LONG DISTANCE CALL FOR YOU!
OH, I HOPE IT'S SPEED!

PHONE
BUS S
I'LL BE ALL RIGHT, MOM! I'M JUST SORRY I FAILED!
UH? WHAT!? ARE YOU SURE YOU'RE NOT DREAMING? THAT'S GREAT!
PHONE
IF I HURRY, THERE MIGHT STILL BE TIME TO KEEP THE MACH 5 FROM BEING SOLD!
DEPARTURE
BUT AFTER A MAD DASH ACROSS MANHATTAN AND PAST CROTHEBY'S SECURITY GUARDS...
SOLD!
FOR $700,000 TO--
--CAPT. QUINN VAN SCOTT!
AT LAST, SPEED--YOUR FABULOUS CAR BELONGS TO ME!
AND I DIDN'T EVEN HAVE TO STEAL IT!
13
OH, NO!
NEXT ISSUE:
THE QUEST FOR THE MACH V

Speed Racer #31

SPEED RACER
TROUBLE IN PARADISE
SPEED RACER HAS DRIVEN THE FABULOUS MACH 5 TO VICTORY IN DOZENS OF RACES AROUND THE WORLD. BUT AFTER HIS FATHER WAS DUPED IN A CROOKED BUSINESS DEAL, THE MACH 5 WAS SOLD TO THE HIGHEST BIDDER!
LAMAR WALDRON STORY
NORM DWYER PENCILS
BRIAN THOMAS INKS
JOSEPH ALLEN LETTERS/COLORS
MICHELE MACH ART DIRECTOR
KATHERINE LLEWELLYN EDITOR
TONY CAPUTO EDITOR-IN-CHIEF
SPEED'S OLD ENEMY, THE NOTORIOUS PIRATE CAPT. QUINN VAN SCOTT, WON THE BIDDING... AND NOW SHE'S TRYING TO TAKE POSSESSION OF THE CAR BEFORE SPEED CAN TAKE LEGAL ACTION TO STOP HER!
CROTHEBY'S
NO PARKING 24 HOUR LOADING ZONE
DON'T YOU UNDERSTAND, SPEED? I WANT YOU AS WELL AS YOUR CAR!
COME ALONG QUIETLY-- IT'S THE ONLY WAY YOU'LL EVER GET TO DRIVE THE MACH 5 AGAIN!
NOT ON YOUR LIFE, VAN SCOTT! AND I WON'T LET YOU TAKE MY CAR-- UUFF!
COVER BY NORM DWYER AND BRIAN THOMAS

DARN IT... HERE COMES A COP! THE POLICE MUST HAVE REALIZED WHO I AM!
ACME DISPOSAL
QUICK--CLIMB ABOARD! WE'VE GOT TO GET BACK TO THE SUB!
YES, CAPTAIN!

FAREWELL, SPEED! IT'S A SHAME YOU WON'T BE COMING WITH US, BUT I CAN ASSURE YOU THAT WE'LL MEET AGAIN!

MY FAMILY... I'VE FAILED THEM! IT'S BEEN HARD ENOUGH FOR POPS TO DEAL WITH HIS HEART ATTACK...
...BUT WHAT WILL HAPPEN TO HIM WHEN HE FINDS OUT THE MACH 5 IS GONE, FOREVER!

TOO DIZZY TO STAND UP! IS IT BECAUSE OF THAT LAST PUNCH... OR FROM EXHAUSTION?
CAN'T REMEMBER THE LAST TIME I SLEPT OR HAD ANY FOOD...
I HOPE THE POOR BOY IS ALL RIGHT! IT'S ALL MY FAULT-- I THOUGHT MY AUCTION HOUSE WAS DEALING WITH THE CAR'S REAL OWNER!

IT'S JUST A SHAME WE DIDN'T RECOGNIZE CAPT. VAN SCOTT SOONER-- SHE'S WANTED FOR PIRACY IN THIRTY COUNTRIES!
SPEED--ARE YOU ALL RIGHT? DON'T TRY TO MOVE!
WHAT'S HAPPENING? EVERYTHING'S SHIFTING-- CHANGING--

ON A BEACH IN THE U.S. VIRGIN ISLANDS...
SPEED--WAKE UP! YOU'RE HAVING A NIGHTMARE!
UH? WHAT HAPPENED TO NEW YORK--ALL THE SNOW?
THERE'S ONLY SAND AND BLUE SKY HERE, OLD PAL!

DON'T YOU REMEMBER? AFTER THE AUCTION, WE CAME TO MY PARENTS' SO YOU AND POPS COULD RECUPERATE!
IT'S ALL COMING BACK TO ME NOW, TRIXIE!

YOU KNOW, I WISH ALL THE PROBLEMS THAT CROOK SAM MOORE CAUSED WERE JUST A DREAM! POP'S HEART ATTACK, BEING KICKED OUT OF OUR HOME, LOSING THE MACH 5--
I'M AFRAID THEY'RE ONLY TOO REAL! BUT THANKS TO ALL YOUR FRIENDS, POPS IS BACK ON HIS FEET--

--AND YOUR FAMILY HAS PLENTY OF MONEY TO BUILD ANOTHER RACE CAR!
I'M REALLY GRATEFUL FOR EVERYONE'S HELP-- BUT NOTHING CAN EVER REPLACE THE MACH 5!

I KNOW HOW YOU FEEL, SPEED. I'LL REALLY MISS WORKING ON HER! BUT LIFE HAS TO GO ON!
YOU'VE GOT TO PUT IT OUT OF YOUR MIND!
GO
I'LL TRY, SPARKY!

MEANWHILE, BACK AT THE BEACH HOUSE, POPS AND MOM ARE TALKING WITH TRIXIE'S PARENTS...
I CAN'T THANK YOU FOLKS ENOUGH FOR ALL YOU'VE DONE!
ARE YOU SURE WE'RE NOT IMPOSING?
DON'T BE RIDICULOUS! WE ENJOY HAVING GUESTS, ISN'T THAT RIGHT, DEARY?
YES, DEAR!

I JUST WISH WE HADN'T BEEN AWAY ON THAT EXPEDITION WHEN YOU WERE HAVING ALL THAT TROUBLE! WE COULD HAVE KEPT YOU FROM--
NOW, DEAR, LET'S NOT DWELL ON THE PAST! THE RACER FAMILY CAME HERE TO FORGET ABOUT THEIR PROBLEMS AND RELAX!

YOU'RE RIGHT AS USUAL, SWEETIE!
AND TO TAKE YOUR MIND OFF THINGS, THERE'S NOTHING BETTER THAN A PARTY!
IN FACT, I'M THROWING A LITTLE SOIREE TONIGHT--

--SO YOU CAN MEET OUR NEIGHBORS HERE ON ST. THOMAS. I'VE ALSO INVITED SOME FRIENDS WHO ARE HERE ON A CRUISE!
IT'LL BE A SMALL PARTY--ONLY A HUNDRED GUESTS!
I CAN HARDLY BELIEVE IT! JUST A FEW WEEKS AGO, WE HAD TO MOVE INTO A HOMELESS SHELTER...
AND NOW, WE'RE LIVING LIKE ROYALTY!

NOT FAR OFFSHORE, THE PASSENGERS OF A CRUISE SHIP DEPART FOR A DAY OF FUN ON ST. THOMAS...
EXCUSE ME, MISS--

DID YOU MISS THE SHUTTLE BOATS? ALL THE OTHER PASSENGERS HAVE ALREADY LEFT FOR THE ISLAND!
BUT I'D BE HAPPY TO TAKE YOU ASHORE IN THE CAPTAIN'S BOAT!
THAT WON'T BE NECESSARY! YOU SEE, I DON'T LIKE CROWDS!

I'VE BEEN WAITING FOR SOME TIME!
WELL, LET ME KNOW IF THERE'S ANYTHING YOU NEED!

IT'S A SHAME THERE'S A RULE AGAINST DATING PASSENGERS...
SNAP!

PARDON ME, SIR--
YES, MISS?

ONE OF MY BACK STRAPS HAS SNAPPED! I CAN'T HOLD MY SUIT TOGETHER AND TIE IT AT THE SAME TIME!
CAN YOU HELP ME WITH IT?
YES, MA'AM!

JUST A FEW MORE SECONDS, AND I THINK I'LL GET IT--
YOU KNOW, I DO BELIEVE YOU'RE RIGHT!

UUUGGHH!
POK!
EXCELLENT, BRUNO!

QUICK-- DRAG HIM INTO THE OFFICE, BEFORE ANYONE ELSE COMES BY!
YES, CAPTAIN!

HERE ARE THE KEYS TO THE SAFE! NOW START LOADING UP ALL THE JEWELRY AND CASH!

THAT'S ENOUGH! SOMEONE'S COMING!

STOP! PUT THAT DOWN!
PITCH IT, BRUNO!

COME ON, BOYS--
OVER THE SIDE!

SPLASH!

SHALL I CALL THE COAST GUARD?
OF COURSE! AND LOWER ONE OF THE BOATS -- THOSE THIEVES WILL HAVE TO COME UP FOR AIR SOONER OR LATER!

FAR BELOW THE CRUISE SHIP, CAPT. SCOTT AND HER MEN HEAD TOWARD HER SUBMA- RINE, THE ATLANTIS...

ATTENTION, MEN! PREPARE TO MOVE FAR- THER OFFSHORE! WE'RE NOT LEAVING THE ISLANDS YET, BUT WE DON'T WANT ANY PATROL SHIPS TO SPOT US!

MEANWHILE...
TRIXIE, I'D LIKE TO SEE IF INSPECTOR DETECTOR HAS ANY NEWS! WOULD YOU MIND IF I MAKE A LONG DISTANCE TELEPHONE CALL?
GO RIGHT AHEAD! YOU CAN USE THE PHONE IN MY BEDROOM!

YES, OPERATOR, I'D LIKE YOU TO CONNECT ME WITH INTERPOL HEADQUARTERS IN NEW YORK!

WITHIN MOMENTS, SPEED IS ON THE LINE WITH INSPECTOR DETECTOR...
I'M AFRAID OUR SURVEILLANCE SATELLITES LOST CAPT. SCOTT'S SUBMARINE WHEN IT ENTERED THE CARIBBEAN!
BUT DON'T WORRY-- I'M HEADING DOWN TO THAT AREA MYSELF, TO TAKE CHARGE OF THE SEARCH! AND SPEED--

I THOUGHT YOU'D LIKE TO KNOW THAT SAM MOORE WAS ARRESTED YESTERDAY!
TURNS OUT HE WAS WORKING FOR DILLIN'S DRUG SMUGGLING RING!

IT FIGURES! I JUST HOPE THAT CROOK GETS WHAT HE DESERVES! OH, AND THANKS AGAIN FOR ALL YOUR HELP, INSPECTION! YOU'RE A REAL PAL!

ANY LUCK?
THEY'VE LOST TRACK OF CAPT. VAN SCOTT! BUT SAM MOORE IS FINALLY IN JAIL -- HE WAS WORKING FOR DILLIN ALL THE TIME!

I HOPE THEY KEEP HIM BEHIND BARS FOR A LONG TIME!
ME, TOO! BUT NO MATTER WHAT THEY DO TO HIM, IT WON'T BRING BACK THE MACH 5!

OH, SPEED-- DON'T TORTURE YOURSELF! POPS CAN BUILD ANOTHER ONE!
YOU DON'T UNDERSTAND, TRIXIE!

POPS DESIGNED THE MACH 5-- BUT HE COULDN'T HAVE BUILT IT WITHOUT MY BROTHER, REX!

IT'S BEEN YEARS SINCE REX DISAPPEARED!
THE MACH 5 WAS MY LAST LINK TO HIM-- AND NOW, IT'S GONE! WHAT'S THE USE OF RACING IF I CAN'T DRIVE THE MACH 5 ?!

OH, SPEED-- YOU CAN'T GIVE UP! YOU LOVE RACING! WHAT WOULD REX THINK IF HE EVER HEARD YOU TALKING LIKE THIS?
MAYBE YOU'RE RIGHT, TRIXIE!

AN HOUR LATER, ABOARD THE ATLANTIS...
THERE WAS ONLY A HUNDRED THOUSAND DOLLARS IN CASH, CAPTAIN. BUT THANKS TO A COUPLE OF LARGE DIAMOND NECKLACES, THE JEWELRY CAN BE FENCED FOR AT LEAST TWICE THAT!
BAH! THAT'S BARELY ENOUGH TO BUY US PROVISIONS FOR A MONTH! I'LL NEED TO PULL SOME HEISTS ON LAND TO GET SOME REAL MONEY!
WHAT ABOUT THE MACH 5, JEFF? HAVE THE MECHANICS GOT IT RUNNING, YET?
NO, SIR, THEY'RE STILL HAVING PROBLEMS WITH THE COMPUTERIZED IGNITION SYSTEM!
BLAST IT!! THEY'VE BEEN WORKING ON IT FOR WEEKS! COME ON, LET'S GET TO THE BOTTOM OF THIS!
SORRY, CAPTAIN, BUT IT'S NOT LIKE ANY CAR I'VE EVER SEEN! IT'S IMPOSSIBLE TO FIGURE OUT!

THEY CAN DESIGN AND BUILD A SUBMARINE -- BUT THEY CAN'T EVEN GET A CAR STARTED!

IT LOOKS LIKE I'LL HAVE TO GET SPEED IF I WANT TO USE THAT CAR!
THE CAPTAIN IS REALLY STUCK ON THIS SPEED RACER FELLOW. IF ONLY SHE FELT THE SAME WAY ABOUT ME!..

MEANWHILE...
TRIXIE, COULD YOU DRIVE INTO TOWN TO PICK UP SOME EXTRA SUPPLIES FOR THE PARTY?
SURE, MOTHER!
MIND IF I GO ALONG?

MINUTES LATER...
IT'S SPEED-- AND HIS GIRLFRIEND, TRIXIE! THEY WON'T STAND A CHANCE OF OUTRUNNING US IN THAT OLD JEEP!

CALLING CAPTAIN VAN SCOTT!
WE'RE GETTING INTO POSITION AND WILL AT-TACK WHEN SPEED PASSES THIS WAY AGAIN!

ROBIN & EDWARD'S ALL AMERICAN DISCO
GEE, WHAT'S ALL THE COMMOTION ABOUT?
I OVERHEARD SOME OF THE PAS-SENGERS TALKING IN THE STORE!
THEIR SHIP WAS **ROBBED**!
BUCKS

SO YOU REALLY LIKE THE VIRGIN ISLANDS?
YEAH--IT'S SO QUIET AND PEACEFUL!

HOLY COW! WHAT WAS THAT?!
BUCKS
VROOOOOM!

I DON'T LIKE THE LOOKS OF THIS! THOSE WERE NO ORDINARY JOY-RIDERS!
THERE'S SOME-THING FISHY GOING ON!

HERE THEY COME AGAIN! I'VE NEVER SEEN ARMORED MOTORCYCLES LIKE THAT! WHAT DO THEY WANT?

SPEED OUGHT TO BE REALLY RATTLED BY NOW! LET'S RUN 'EM OFF THE ROAD!

SPEED--LOOK OUT!

HOLD TIGHT, TRIXIE! THIS JEEP MAY NOT BE THE **MACH 5**, BUT I'M GOING TO DO MY BEST TO OUT-MANEUVER THEM!

OH, NO!
DON'T WORRY, SPEED. I'M ALL RIGHT!
OKAY, YOU TWO-- WHAT DO YOU WANT?
THERE'S SOME-ONE WHO WANTS TO SEE YOU--

HEY--A CAR'S COMING! IT MIGHT BE THE **COPS**!
WE'D BETTER **CLEAR OUT** BEFORE WE'RE SPOTTED, OR THE **CAPTAIN** WILL HAVE OUR **HIDE**!
VROOO

MOMENTS LATER...
CAN YOU GIVE US A LIFT?
SURE--**HOP IN!** WE'RE RENT-ING A BEACH HOUSE RIGHT NEXT TO YOUR PLACE!

THAT EVENING...
WHAT'S THAT? INSPECTOR DETECTOR HAS ALREADY LEFT?
WELL, IF HE CALLS IN FOR HIS MESSAGES, PLEASE TELL HIM TO CALL SPEED RACER AS SOON AS POSSIBLE!

SORRY I'M LATE--
OH, SPEED, WAIT UNTIL YOU HEAR THE DETAILS OF THE ROBBERY!
THEY CLEANED OUT ALL THE JEWELRY IN THE SHIP'S SAFE--AND THEN JUMPED OVERBOARD!

THAT SOUNDS ALMOST AS WEIRD AS WHAT HAPPENED TO US TODAY!
I WONDER IF THERE'S SOME CONNECTION?
WE'LL TALK TO THE POLICE ABOUT IT, TOMORROW! FOR NOW, JUST TRY TO RELAX AND HAVE FUN!

GOLLY, CHIM-CHIM, THIS IS AWFUL! THERE'S NO CANDY, NO PRESENTS--
HOW CAN GROWNUPS CALL THIS A PARTY?!

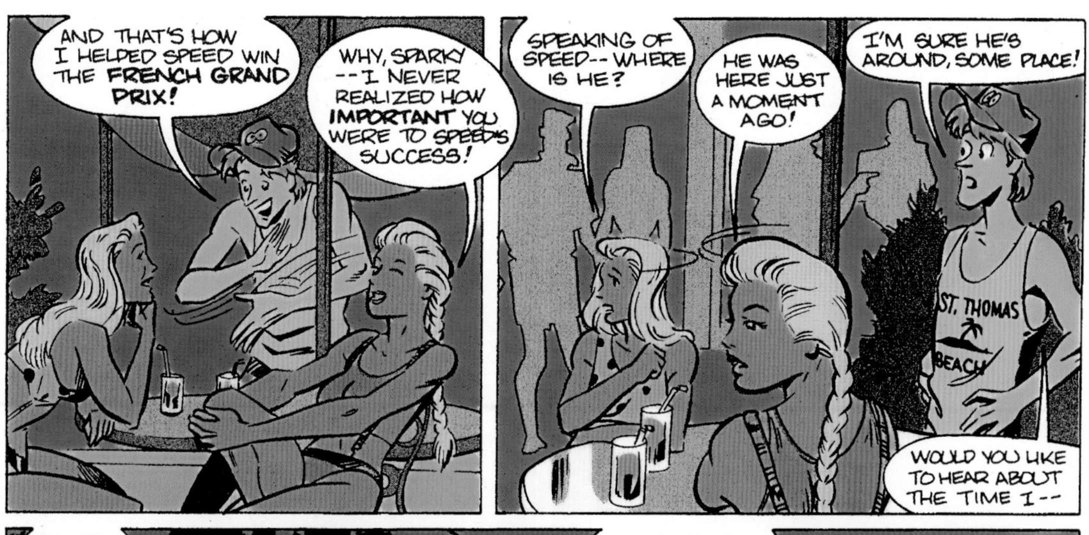
AND THAT'S HOW I HELPED SPEED WIN THE **FRENCH GRAND PRIX!**
WHY, SPARKY --I NEVER REALIZED HOW **IMPORTANT** YOU WERE TO SPEED'S SUCCESS!
SPEAKING OF SPEED-- WHERE IS HE?
HE WAS HERE JUST A MOMENT AGO!
I'M SURE HE'S AROUND, SOME PLACE!
ST. THOMAS BEACH
WOULD YOU LIKE TO HEAR ABOUT THE TIME I--

WHERE ARE WE GOING?
UNLIKE MY MOTHER, I HATE PARTIES! SO I THOUGHT WE'D SLIP AWAY--

--FOR A ROMANTIC MOONLIGHT SWIM!

COME ON IN! THE WATER'S FINE!

MOMENTS LATER...
BRRR-- THIS WATER'S **COLD!**
YOU'LL GET USED TO IT!

GULP!-- THAT WAVE-- SWEPT ME OFF MY FEET!
DON'T WORRY, I'LL CATCH YOU!

SEE-- I TOLD YOU I'D CATCH YOU!
YOU SURE DID! AND YOU KNOW-- I'M NOT THE LEAST BIT COLD, ANYMORE!

HI GUYS! WE'VE COME TO PLAY IN THE SAND, TOO!
SPRIDLE!
CHIM-CHIM!

DON'T YOU KNOW IT'S NOT POLITE TO INTERRUPT?

COME ON! YOU'RE GOING BACK TO THE HOUSE RIGHT NOW!
DON'T WORRY, TRIXIE-- I'LL BE RIGHT HERE!

MOMENTS LATER...
THERE'S SOMETHING OUT IN THE SURF-- CAN'T MAKE OUT WHAT IT IS...

...BUT IT'S COMING THIS WAY!

HELLO, SPEED! PLEASE EXCUSE MY DRAMATIC ENTRANCE-- BUT YOU WOULDN'T ACCOMPANY THE TWO MEN I SENT TO BRING YOU TO ME!

SO YOU WERE BEHIND THAT! WE COULD HAVE BEEN KILLED!
THAT'S NOT WHAT I WANTED, I ASSURE YOU! I ONLY WANTED YOU TO COME TO MY SUBMARINE! I HATE TO SAY THIS ABOUT ANY MAN--

--BUT I NEED YOU, SPEED! THE MACH 5 IS NO GOOD WITHOUT YOU! MY SPECIALTY IS NAUTICAL ENGINEERING--NOT AUTOMOBILES!

I NEED YOU TO REPAIR THE MACH 5, AND BE MY DRIVER ON MY BRIEF TRIPS ASHORE!
IN RETURN, YOU CAN HAVE WEALTH--ADVENTURE--POWER--

--AND ME! THINK OF IT, SPEED--TOGETHER, ANYTHING WE WANT ON LAND OR SEA CAN BE OURS!

MINUTES LATER...
SPEED! SPEED! WHERE ARE YOU?

SUDDENLY...
W-WHAT'S GOING ON? WHERE'S SPEED?
THAT'S WHAT WE'D LIKE TO KNOW! INSPECTOR DETECTOR SENT US DOWN HERE...
...TO KEEP AN EYE ON SPEED!

MINUTES LATER, ON BOARD THE NAUTILUS...
THE MACH 5! I THOUGHT I'D NEVER SEE IT AGAIN!
I'VE TAKEN GOOD CARE OF YOUR PRECIOUS CAR, SPEED-- AND WITH IT, WE CAN TRAVEL THE WORLD TOGETHER!

YOU SEE, SPEED, LIFE UNDERWATER CAN BECOME TOO CONFINING! BUT SINCE I'M A WANTED CRIMINAL, I DARE NOT GO ASHORE FOR VERY LONG!

ONCE YOU HAVE THE MACH 5 RUNNING PROPERLY, I CAN GO ASHORE AT WILL! WITH YOUR DRIVING SKILLS, THE POLICE WILL NEVER BE ABLE TO CATCH US!

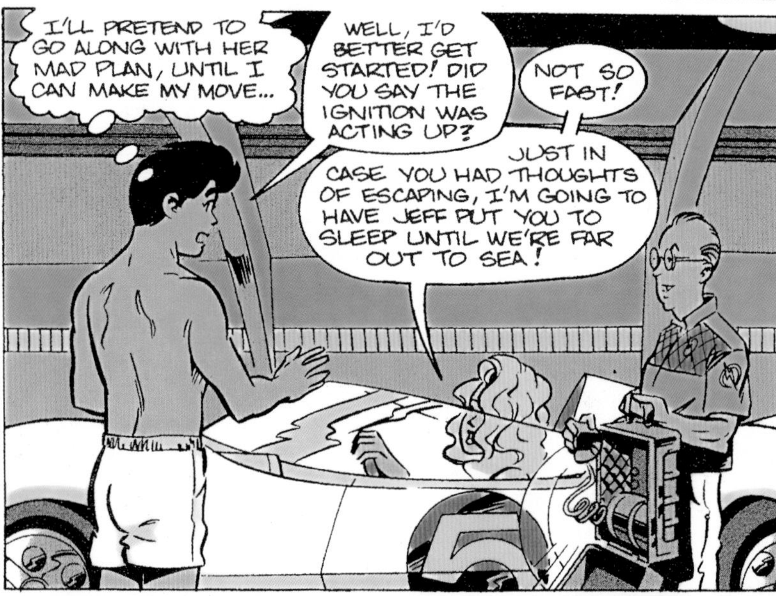
I'LL PRETEND TO GO ALONG WITH HER MAD PLAN, UNTIL I CAN MAKE MY MOVE...
WELL, I'D BETTER GET STARTED! DID YOU SAY THE IGNITION WAS ACTING UP?
NOT SO FAST!
JUST IN CASE YOU HAD THOUGHTS OF ESCAPING, I'M GOING TO HAVE JEFF PUT YOU TO SLEEP UNTIL WE'RE FAR OUT TO SEA!

DON'T WORRY-- THIS WON'T HURT A BIT!
THIS IS MY ONLY CHANCE... BUT I'LL HAVE TO TAKE BOTH OF THEM OUT BEFORE THEY CAN SOUND AN ALARM!

SORRY PAL, BUT IT'S NOT MY BEDTIME!
OWWW! LET GO!

FOOL! YOU'LL RUIN EVERYTHING!

IF I CAN'T HAVE YOU--NO ONE WILL!
CAN'T BREATHE ... JUST ONE WAY TO STOP HER...
SSSSSSSS

UHHHH...

CALLING FOR REINFORCEMENTS? YOU'LL NEED 'EM, BECAUSE I'M GOING TO FIGHT TO THE BITTER END FOR THE MACH 5!
SUCH BRAVADO IS UNCALLED FOR--AND QUITE UNNECESSARY!
AIRLOCK 5

YOU SEE, I'M NOT CALLING THE GUARDS--I'M OPENING THE AIRLOCK SO YOU CAN ESCAPE!

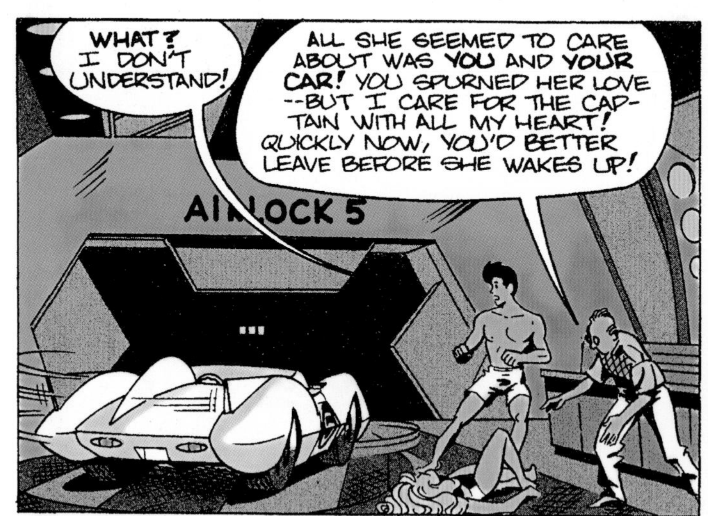
AIRLOCK 5
WHAT? I DON'T UNDERSTAND!
ALL SHE SEEMED TO CARE ABOUT WAS YOU AND YOUR CAR! YOU SPURNED HER LOVE --BUT I CARE FOR THE CAPTAIN WITH ALL MY HEART! QUICKLY NOW, YOU'D BETTER LEAVE BEFORE SHE WAKES UP!

I JUST HOPE THE IGNITION PROBLEM ISN'T TOO SERIOUS-- OR WE'LL BOTH BE IN BIG TROUBLE!

MINUTES LATER...
IT FEELS GREAT TO BE BEHIND THE WHEEL AGAIN! I'M GLAD A SIMPLE WIRING SWITCH WAS ALL THE IGNITION NEEDED!
AS SOON AS I CLOSE THE CANOPY AND ACTIVATE MY OXYGEN SUPPLY, I'LL BE ALL SET!

MEANWHILE, INSPECTOR DETECTOR HAS FINALLY ARRIVED ON ST. THOMAS, TO JOIN THE SEARCH FOR SPEED AND CAPTAIN VAN SCOTT...
THAT'S RIGHT, I WANT ALL COAST GUARD SHIPS IN THE AREA TO BE COMBING THE AREA IMMEDIATELY!

SUDDENLY...

OH, SPEED-- I'M SO GLAD YOU'RE SAFE! BUT HOW DID YOU ESCAPE?
THE MACH 5 CAME THROUGH AGAIN -- JUST LIKE IT ALWAYS DOES!
THE END!

VROOM
RRRR
WRROOMMM

VVROOM